Loving someone who struggles with mental hea... ... ... conscripted to ride a terrifying rollercoaster in the dark — you have no idea when or if the ride will end, and you never chose to ride the rollercoaster in the first place! Step off of the rollercoaster, and instead grab this book, *Holding on to Hope–Staying Sane While Loving Someone with a Mental Illness*. Pastor Brad Hoefs of Fresh Hope for Mental Health and his wife Donna will show you a way forward that offers practical insight, helpful ideas, dignity, choice, and clear scriptural inspiration for living well in spite of mental illness, instead of life as a victim of your loved one's diagnosis. Learn to walk alongside your loved one more effectively in spite of their mental illness, and in spite of your own pain and challenges. Most of all, there is hope – real, solid, attainable hope. You and your loved one can find hope for wellness and a better future together.

**Tara Rolstad, Mental Health Speaker and Author**
**Founder of Shattering Stigma with Stories, <u>tararolstad.com</u>**


If your loved one suffers with mental illness, then *Holding to Hope* will speak directly to you. Brad and Donna Hoefs use their story of lived experience and realistic examples as they navigate readers through challenging emotions and self-reflection. Loving someone with mental illness can be lonely and can leave you feeling hopeless, but this book validates the struggle and frustration while painting a future of hope and recovery. Reading this book will encourage and connect you to a community of people who feel just like you and offer you the support that you are longing for.

**Laura Howe**
**BSW, RSW, CAPM**

# HOLDING *to* HOPE

*Staying Sane While Loving Someone with a Mental Illness*

BRAD & DONNA HOEFS

XULON PRESS ELITE

Xulon Press Elite
2301 Lucien Way #415
Maitland, FL 32751
407.339.4217
www.xulonpress.com

© 2021 by Brad & Donna Hoefs

All rights reserved solely by the author. The author guarantees all contents are original and do not infringe upon the legal rights of any other person or work. No part of this book may be reproduced in any form without the permission of the author. The views expressed in this book are not necessarily those of the publisher.

Due to the changing nature of the Internet, if there are any web addresses, links, or URLs included in this manuscript, these may have been altered and may no longer be accessible. The views and opinions shared in this book belong solely to the author and do not necessarily reflect those of the publisher. The publisher therefore disclaims responsibility for the views or opinions expressed within the work.

Unless otherwise indicated, Scripture quotations taken from the Holy Bible, New International Version (NIV). Copyright © 1973, 1978, 1984, 2011 by Biblica, Inc.™. Used by permission. All rights reserved.

Scripture quotations taken from the Good News Translation (GNT). Copyright © 1992 American Bible Society. Used by permission. All rights reserved.

Scripture quotations taken from the Gods Word Translation. Copyright ©1995 by Baker Publishing Group. Used by permission. All rights reserved.

Paperback ISBN-13: 978-1-6628-1826-4
Ebook ISBN-13: 978-1-6628-1827-1

# Table of Contents

**Acknowledgements** . . . . . . . . . . . . . . . . . . . . . . . . . . . . . . . . . . . . . . . . . . . ix
**Foreword** . . . . . . . . . . . . . . . . . . . . . . . . . . . . . . . . . . . . . . . . . . . . . . . . . . . xiii
**Introduction** . . . . . . . . . . . . . . . . . . . . . . . . . . . . . . . . . . . . . . . . . . . . . . . . . xv
**The Fresh Hope® Principles for Loved Ones** . . . . . . . . . . . . . . . . . . . . xix

## Part 1

**Processing the Principles** . . . . . . . . . . . . . . . . . . . . . . . . . . . . . . . . . . . . . 1
  *Practical Insights for Staying Sane*

Chapter 1
**When Mental Illness Disrupts Your Life** . . . . . . . . . . . . . . . . . . . . . . . . . 3
  *The Brain–Mind Difference*

Chapter 2
**Can My Loved One Recover?** . . . . . . . . . . . . . . . . . . . . . . . . . . . . . . . . . 9
  *Mental Health Recovery: A Hope and a Future*

Chapter 3
**Believe It or Not: There Is Hope** . . . . . . . . . . . . . . . . . . . . . . . . . . . . . . 24
  *When the Feelings of Hopelessness Overshadow the Reality of Hope*

Chapter 4
**You Can't Do This Alone** . . . . . . . . . . . . . . . . . . . . . . . . . . . . . . . . . . . . 40
  *So Don't Try to Do It Alone!*

**Chapter 5**
**Relationships Matter** .................................................51
*Being a Healthy You Helps the Relationship*

**Chapter 6**
**Learn How to Contribute in Appropriate and Healthy Ways** ..........63
*Some Things Help and Other Things Don't Help:*
*Knowing the Difference is Key*

**Chapter 7**
**Set Boundaries and Choose Hope** ....................................74
*Hope is a Choice In Spite of the Circumstances*

**Chapter 8**
**Your Loved One Needs A Healthy and Encouraging You** ...............88
*Become the Best You Possible*

**Chapter 9**
**Healed Heart Wounds Will Allow You to Move Forward** ...............99
*Don't Let the Wounds Fester*

**Chapter 10**
**Giving Back Will Give Back to You** ................................111
*Giving Back Creates Thriving in Spite of Your Circumstances*

**Chapter 11**
**Resiliency in Suffering Which is Rooted in Hope** ..................124
*Apostle Paul's Insights on Resiliency*

**Chapter 12**
**Choosing Hope in the Face of Hopelessness** ........................134
*In Christ, Hopelessness is a Feeling and Hope is a Reality*

## Part 2
**Helpful Hints** .................................................. 147
*For When Holding to Hope is Hard to Do*

## Part 2A
**Living Well** .................................................... 149

**Chapter 13**
Life is 10% What Happens to You and 90% How You React to It ...... 151

**Chapter 14**
Wisdom for Living Well: Knowing the Difference Between
What We Can Change and What We Can't Change .................. 154

**Chapter 15**
We Are Not All the Same ......................................... 158

**Chapter 16**
Medicine is Not a Magic Potion ................................... 161

**Chapter 17**
Warning Signs of Potential Relapse ............................... 165

**Chapter 18**
Perfection vs. Imperfect Progress ................................. 169

## Part 2B
**Relationships** .................................................. 173

**Chapter 19**
What Empowers Your Loved One Vs. What Enables Them .......... 175

**Chapter 20**
Creative 'Non-Confrontive' Ways to Confront Your Loved One ....... 182

**Chapter 21**
**When You Are the Spouse** ................................................. 186

**Chapter 22**
**Learning to Trust Again** ................................................... 190

**Chapter 23**
**When Children Are Involved** .............................................. 194

**Chapter 24**
**When Your Child or Teen Has a Mental Illness** ..................... 198

**Chapter 25**
**When Your Loved One is Suicidal** ...................................... 205

**Chapter 26**
**When "I" Becomes "We" Wellness Happens** ........................ 213

**Chapter 27**
**30 Things You Can Do When Someone You Love
is Clinically Depressed** .................................................... 216

**Chapter 28**
**The Power of Peers Helping Peers** ..................................... 219

**Recommended Resources** ................................................. 223

# Acknowledgements

Sometimes in life, the things we become experienced in choose us. Such is the case with mental illness and loving someone with a mental illness in our lives. For whatever reason, the Lord has allowed us to become well-versed with mental illness and learning to love well someone with a mental health issue.

For both Donna and me, we each had a parent who had a mental illness in the 'old days' when you didn't talk about it, and God forbid that you would talk openly about it. Donna's mother and my father each had bipolar disorder (at the time, it was called manic depression). We watched as our parents navigated the episodes while learning to love each other well despite the mental health challenges they were living through as a couple. Seeing it play out in front of us, at times we learned what worked, but we also learned what did not work. Plus, as children and adults, we have had to learn how to love someone with a mental health issue.

Of course, our experience has also included my own diagnosis and an excruciatingly public manic episode in 1995. It was at that point that Donna got her 'doctoral degree' in being a loved one. Without her, I would not have made it. I believe that I would not be here today had it not been for her loving me well through the time I suffered from the most severe period of having bipolar disorder. During that time, Donna held to hope. She held to the hope that I could recover and that the Lord could take all of the pain and brokenness and turn it into good. Her tightly holding onto hope gave me the strength and courage to begin to hope again.

Through the years, we have continued learning and growing in holding to hope for those who have a mental health issue within our circle of family and friends. And since 2009, when I started Fresh Hope's first group, up to now, we have become 'super-learners' in how to best love someone who has a mental illness. Shortly after starting the first Fresh Hope group, it became evident that those who were loved ones needed encouragement and support as well. So we re-wrote the tenets to include recovery tenets for loved ones. And through the years since, we have seen those tenets provide hope, encouragement, and insight for those who love someone with a mental health issue.

In this book, we offer to you that which we have learned both firsthand and by observation through the years. You are so important in your loved one's mental health journey. We hope to empower you to hold tightly to healing and hope through what we have learned and experienced. We pray that you will gain insights, strength, courage, and healing as you read these pages. Your loved one needs you to stay 'sane' (being as emotionally well and available as possible) as you take this journey with them. We think of hope as being the lighted lantern that you hold onto as you take each step in the darkness of a journey such as this. We pray that you will continue holding to hope (the lantern), keeping it lit with the courage, hope, healing, and strength you find within these pages.

This book has been an arduous task for us. It has required time and reflection, some of which were painful to visit once again. Thank you, Donna, for being willing to take the journey with me so that others might benefit and gain insight from how you have loved me through my worst.

## Acknowledgements

We also want to thank our editor, Julie Koenemann, a dear friend and gifted editor. We thank the Lord for you. This would not have been achievable without you!

Also, a huge thank you to all in our circle of family and friends who have been on this journey with us. Because of your holding to hope for us, you have given us courage, strength, and hope. Your friendships and love have provided healing.

Our journeys with mental illness began when we were children and continued into our adult years. In spite of the mental health diagnosis back in the days of even greater shame and stigma around mental illnesses, our parents still gave us what we needed and loved us unconditionally. And while we lost Donna's mom, Stella, to suicide, we were always shown the true hope we have in Christ Jesus.

Today three of our four parents are with the Lord. My mom, Janelle, is the only one left of the four. Her strength and perseverance continue to give us deep insights into holding to hope for those we love.

Thus, we dedicate the book to our parents: Preston and Stella Smith, and David and Janelle Hoefs. Through all of you, we received the unconditional love and strength that has been necessary for this journey that the Lord has us on.

We also dedicate this book to our siblings, who, in fact, lived through our parents' mental health journey, too: Donna's brothers: Joe, David, and Keith; and my sister, Brenda. We love you guys and your spouses! You have been such blessings to us through some of our darkest days and nights!

And finally, we dedicate this book to our children, Noah and Noelle. Just like Donna and me, their journey with mental illness started in childhood. They each lived through the worst of it altogether. And while there were hurts and pains, they experienced what we wish they would not have had to deal with. They are persevering and have great compassion for others because of all they have been through themselves. In spite of some parental 'fails', you two have turned out to be loving, caring, and faith-filled adults. We are proud to call you our son and our daughter.

Brad Hoefs
Holy Week 2021

# Foreword

**H**olding to Hope is a book about finding hope when none appears in the surrounding circumstances. While it records many examples from all walks of life, it is principally the struggle Pastor Brad Hoefs and his wife, Donna, have faced and overcome during the past twenty-five years since he was first diagnosed with bipolar disorder. The condition can present with mood swings, either up or down, sometimes one following the other. In Brad's illness, initial mania was followed by a long period of depression worsened by loss of position and professional relationships. His wife Donna has supported, encouraged, assisted, and held him accountable throughout.

In my professional practice as a psychiatrist, I have been privileged to work with Brad and Donna the entire twenty-five years. Their situation is not unique, and other forms of mental illness can present the same devasting consequences to both the designated suffer and their loved ones. As a physician, it is my calling to ameliorate their suffering as best I am able. This includes medical treatment and as much wisdom and insight I can muster to guide them on the path to recovery. Recovery does not mean full restoration of all that has been lost, but recovering as much as possible and growing beyond the trauma of mental illness towards a future that might not have been possible without the hurdles mental illness imposes. This process of growth requires overcoming rather than succumbing.

Overcoming requires looking beyond the circumstances at the future and implies hope. Hope in what? Self? Spouse? Life in general? God? This brings us to ***Holding***

***to Hope***. It recognizes that everyone has pain, losses, and tragedies in their lives. Whether it is the loss of a love one, financial collapse, divorce, or mental illness. You either work through it or get stuck in it. As the old adage goes, life is 10% what happens to you and 90% how you react to it. The most appropriate response in the famous Serenity Prayer of Reinhold Niebuhr. (See Chapter 14)

You cannot change that your loved one has a mental illness, how other people react to it, or that they need treatment. You *can* change how you respond to others despite how they may react, seek those who are understanding and supportive, and live life despite loving someone with a mental health challenge. It is only a part of life, not the whole of it.

Michael L. Egger, MD, DLFAP

# Introduction

When it comes to mental illness, it is an equal opportunity provider of pain, struggles, and difficulties. Those who have a mental illness and their loved ones are all subject to the layers of difficulties that mental illness brings into relationships and life itself. There is no doubt in our minds that being the loved one of someone who has a mental illness can be as difficult as having the illness itself. In fact, it is even possible for those who love someone with a mental illness to suffer even more than their loved one who has the diagnosis. It is so very difficult to watch someone you love suffer so much, and even more difficult when they refuse to be compliant in their treatment or they continually self-sabotage their recovery.

The mental illness of someone you love and care about deeply has brought you to a point of picking up this book and opening it to find hope – for the one you love and even for yourself. Their pain is your pain. Their hurt is your hurt. Their struggle is your struggle. Yet intuitively you know that in spite of your own pain, hurt, and struggle, you are a lifeline for the potential recovery of your loved one. So it is through your tears and in spite of the fear of failure that you desire to do your part – and sometimes more than your part – in the recovery of your loved one. Suddenly you are their mental health coach, mental health advocate, life coach, and their overall advocate. And yet, who is caring for you? How do you keep from being 'done in' by the roller coaster of mental health recovery?

How do you find hope in the midst of what seems to be a hopeless situation? How do you as their loved one hold on to hope for them and yourself? How do give them hope much less hold onto hope yourself? That's what this book is about. It's about giving you hope. This book will empower you to hold onto hope while offering hope to your loved one who has a mental illness.

## *What this book is not:*

- It's not a book for telling you what you need to do and not do to bring about wellness for the one you love.
- It's not a book to educate you about the mental health system or educate you about your loved one's mental illness.
- It's not a book to tell you about what to expect with your loved one's illness.
- It's not a book about you fixing what is wrong with your loved one who has a mental illness, nor is it about how you can fix any of it.
- It is not an exhaustive discourse on mental health.

## *Rather, this book is about:*

- Coming alongside you with hope and encouragement as you give care and love to someone who has a mental illness;
- Empowering you to live well in spite of the roller coaster ride of your loved one's mental illness/health;
- Empowering you with some practical and helpful insights;
- Empowering you to care for yourself; and
- Assuring you that you are not alone.

We want you to understand that your healthy support is key in helping and caring for the one you love suffering with a mental health challenge. Please take note, it is your **healthy** support. If *you* are not healthy and at your best, your care and encouragement for your loved one will be lacking. You first need to take care of yourself, or you will be sucked into the pits of despair yourself. Chances are you might be there right now. No one can be 'on' 24/7. You need breaks. You need time for yourself. You need time to recreate. This book is about helping you replenish, refuel, and refresh so that you might be continually renewed. Loving someone with a mental health challenge is more of a marathon than a sprint. And it is an ongoing challenge and hard work that can wear you down and begin to affect your own mental health.

There is no doubt in our minds that being the loved one of someone who has a mental illness is just as painful, and sometimes even more, than the pain of being mentally ill. The recovery journey is difficult. Mental illness affects everyone around the one who has the illness. While the major focus is on the one who has mental health issues, those who love them are feeling the sting, pain, and heart wounds as a result of the disruptive behaviors due to the mental illness. It is life-altering for everyone.

**Your healthy support is key**

And while there are no easy answers or a simple formula to follow, there is good news. There is hope. It's a real, sure and certain hope. It's not wishful-thinking hope. And this hope is not even dependent on whether or not your loved one finds their pathway to living well! *You* can live well and with hope in spite of your loved one's recovery. It doesn't mean you won't feel the pain, but you can work through it and hold onto hope *in spite of* their ups and downs. You can become the hero against the villain of mental illness in your life.

This book is for you, the loved one. Our intent is to empower you to live well, give you hope and the strength to hold onto that hope in spite of the ups and downs of your loved one's recovery journey. We hope to provide you with practical insights, cause you to think, encourage you to find healing, and most of all to assure you that you are NOT alone.

# Two Parts

## Part 1

**Processing the Principles** – *Practical Insights for Staying Sane*

In Part 1, our approach is to guide you through the seven Fresh Hope® Recovery Principles for Loved Ones. As we look at each, we will help you process each principle in a practical way. This becomes your workbook for *staying sane while loving someone who has a mental health diagnosis*. You can work through them by yourself, or you can process them in a small group of loved ones. The chapters on the Recovery Principles are created especially for use in a group setting.

## Part 2

**Helpful Hints** – *For When Holding to Hope is Hard to Do*

In Part 2, we address a number of specific issues that we hear loved ones ask again and again within our groups, in shorter chapters than in Part 1. The first six chapters address topics on Living Well; the final chapters focus on relationships. We'll share with you our experiences as loved ones, and also what we have seen through the collective wisdom of the loved ones we have met through the years. Some of the chapters include simple lists of insights based upon our experience. While you may not find easy answers, what you will discover are insights that hopefully will lead you to creatively pursuing the right answers for you and your loved one.

# The Fresh Hope® Principles for Loved Ones

#1 **My loved one's mental health challenge has also left me feeling helpless and hopeless. Therefore, I choose the help of others in learning about the disorder and choosing healthy boundaries for myself.**

Together, we have understanding. We remind each other of the Lord's love, and that He alone can do all things. He is the source of our hope, and in Him we can overcome all things.

*"I can do everything through Him who gives me strength." Philippians 4:13 (NIV)*

#2 **I haven't always responded to my loved one's mental health issue in ways that were good for the relationship. Therefore, I choose to learn better ways to communicate with, support, and encourage my loved one.**

Together, we commit to speaking the truth in love, healing broken relationships and viewing each other as the Lord views us.

*"So let's pursue those things which bring peace and which are good for each other." Romans 14:19 (God's Word Translation, 1995)*

**#3 At times I don't understand my loved one and can allow them to either wallow in their excuses, or push them too hard. Therefore I choose to learn healthy, appropriate ways to contribute to my loved one's recovery.**

Together we do better than trying on our own. We will hold one another accountable for learning, growing, and choosing to push through in hope.

*"Therefore, encourage one another and build each other up." 1 Thessalonians 5:11 (NIV)*

**#4 At times I also feel hopeless, letting my loved one's actions and recovery define my happiness. Therefore, I choose to live with healthy emotional boundaries, and I choose my own joy despite the ups and downs of my loved one.**

Together we remind each other that our hope and joy come from the Lord. He alone is able to fulfill our needs in every aspect of our lives.

*"For I know the plans I have for you, declares the LORD, plans to prosper you and not to harm you, plans to give you hope and a future." Jeremiah 29:11 (NIV)*

**#5 I, too, have been part of the cycle of dysfunctional living, either thinking I had all the answers or thinking the problem didn't belong to me. Therefore, I choose to submit myself to learning new behaviors and taking responsibility for my own healthy, balanced living.**

Together we choose freedom over suffering, and joy in living through self-knowledge in action.

*"We demolish arguments and every pretension that sets itself up against the knowledge of God and we take captive every thought to make it obedient to Christ." 2 Corinthians 10:5*

**#6** **At times, I have viewed myself as a victim of my loved one's behavior and disorder, living in resentment, anger, unforgiveness, or self-pity. Therefore, I choose to separate the disorder from the person I love, forgive and let go of the past, and live as a contributor to successful recovery.**

Together, we share in each other's victories and celebrate the whole person.

*For God has not given us a spirit of fear, but of power and love and a sound mind." 2 Timothy 1:7*

**#7** **I, too, have become focused on my loved one's situation and how it has affected me. I can easily become so consumed by our issues that I fail to see those around me who would benefit from what I've learned. Therefore, I choose to give back by seeking opportunities to help others by sharing my insights and experiences.**

Together we recognize that sharing helps both us and others heal. Sharing helps us find our voice and becomes empowering as we see our pain redeemed by the Lord. As we share, it helps reaffirm our own hope while also giving hope away to others.

*"(The Lord) helps us in all our troubles, so that we are able to help others who have all kinds of troubles, using the same help that we ourselves have received from God." 2 Corinthians 1:4 (Good News Translation)*

Part 1

# Processing the Principles

*Practical Insights for Staying Sane*

## Chapter 1

# When Mental Illness Disrupts Your Life

*The Brain – Mind Difference*

(Brad)

In 1975, my life, as well as the lives of my entire family, was disrupted, interrupted, and changed forever. What happened? Well, my father had a nervous breakdown (that's what it was called it back then). He had his first episode of depression with his bipolar disorder.

At the time we didn't know it. This was a strong, almost 'thuggish' man with a bad temper, but who could also be lot of fun. He was busy adding on to our house and doing all kinds of things with farming and feeding the cattle, and all of a sudden he became a puddle of tears. It was shocking. I didn't know how to respond to it at all. I was a senior in high school. I was busy living, having a good life, and my father became very withdrawn, wasn't doing anything, and was crying a lot. It was very hush-hush even within our immediate family, and heaven forbid we would talk about it with anybody else. Finally, they got him to a doctor, a psychiatrist who diagnosed him right away and put him on lithium. This disruption took a while and it was painful. And I remember it yet to this day.

If you're reading this book, then there's a good chance that you've experienced a similar kind of disruption in your life. Sometimes the disruption is sudden and unexpected, like with my dad. It was just almost overnight, and it was like, "What happened?" Other times it's like watching the cars collide and crumple in a very slow train wreck. Sometimes the diagnosis finally makes sense of what hasn't made sense for years. Or sometimes it hits like a tragic car accident: suddenly your loved one's mind crashes due to a 'perfect storm' within their life.

It's complex. When mental illness interrupts, it doesn't disrupt in the same way in every case. Like I said, sometimes it's slow; other times it's sudden. But you find yourself asking some of the same questions, like, "What happened? What happened to my loved one? This isn't the way they act. Why are they acting this way? Why can't they change back? Why can't they do something about it?"

After all, behavior is what we see. It's the symptomatic aspect of something that's wrong with the brain. "Why can't they choose to think differently? Why can't they decide to do this? Why are they acting like this? Why can't they just remember what made them happy? Why can't they just get out of this funk?" Well, that behavior is a symptom that their brain is not working properly. And in many cases such as with depression, bipolar disorder, schizophrenia, and schizoaffective disorder, it has to do with brain chemistry. Sometimes it has to do with their thinking, as in thinking disorders. But in any case, it has to do with the brain not functioning properly. For instance, if somebody has PTSD and they've suffered trauma, that trauma and PTSD has most likely changed their brain chemistry.

## *Mind vs. Brain*

It's really important for you to understand as a loved one that this is not something your loved one has chosen, nor is it because they're lazy and aren't doing enough to get over it. Maybe the best way to start with understanding is to know that there's a difference between your mind and your brain.

Scripture tells us that we have the mind of Christ. But if somebody's lost their mind, how is that the mind of Christ? The truth is we do have the mind of Christ, but there are times when someone's brain is not working properly.

Remember that the brain is a physical organ made up of tissue. It's physiological. It's no more spiritual than any other part of your body. Your mind is what your brain does, and that's where the problems show up. It's how the mind thinks, and how people act, that becomes the issue. When your brain doesn't work right, you're not going to be in your right mind, either. If your loved one's brain chemistry is 'off', then what they think, say, and do – how they behave – is affected. That's why in the medical profession, mental health is called *behavioral* health.

Especially in cases with bipolar disorder, schizoaffective disorder, schizophrenia, depression, and even anxiety, people can end up acting like they've been shot up with hallucinogenic drugs, and they're just not themselves. That's what happens to those who have mental health disorders. It's as though somebody comes in the middle of the night and changes their brain chemistry. The brain is not functioning properly. As the loved one, you can be mad about their brain chemistry being off, but not at your loved one. They don't choose how their brain chemistry works, any more than you do.

**Your loved one has not chosen this**

No, your loved one has not chosen this, nor have you. This is not a character flaw for them, but it's going to test both their character and yours. This does not make them less of a person, nor is this a moral issue, or a lack of faith. But your faith is going to be tested. It's as physical as any other illness that we have. Why? Because it has to do with our body. It has to do with the brain. Now, the one choice that your loved one and you can make is to get help, to learn as much as you can about it, and be determined to not let it rob you of life.

How long will it take? Clinical depression may go away after some period of time. If it's chronic clinical depression or major depressive disorder, it may not. And things like bipolar, schizophrenia, schizoaffective disorder – those things are not going to go away. That's why you have to make the choice along with your loved one to learn how to live well in spite of the challenging diagnosis. It's certainly a disruption. But one of the signs of healthy mental health recovery is when a person begins to take their life back. We'll talk about that later. But when people want to begin to live out their life again, as opposed to their mental illness sucking the life out of them and you, that's a good sign. That's a good sign because they're starting to recover.

*A bit of reflection:*

How has mental illness 'disrupted' your life?

_____

_____

_____

_____

What is the difference between your brain and your mind?

_____

_____

_____

_____

## Devotional Reflection

When a crisis in life strikes, such as a mental health crisis, you truly find out what you're made of – and good for you! You're reading a book right now to help you find courage and some direction as you face this crisis. That's a good sign that you are made of some good 'stuff'. You know that you can't go it alone.

When a mental health crisis strikes, you also find out who your friends are. Some will understand. Other friends will be silent out of fear of not knowing what to say or do. They've not gone through anything like it and may not have even gone through a crisis of any kind in life. Love them anyway. It's not because they don't love you; it's because they don't understand. And those who have been broken enough in life and have walked through some type of crisis will be able to walk alongside of you. They'll know how important it is to just be there alongside of you. Love them, and let them walk with you.

And finally, when a crisis in life such as a mental health crisis happens, you find out that the Lord has not gone anywhere. In fact, He draws near. The scriptures tell us that God draws near to the broken-hearted. He is with you every step of the way. He has promised to take all the things that you go through and work them out together *for your good*, and because He loves you and has called you, you are His.

Mental illness has disrupted your life, and it feels like you are walking through hell. Well, don't stop. Keep walking, one step at a time. We hope to help guide you through your journey in the coming pages, that you may come through it stronger, more courageous, and more faith-filled and hope-filled than ever before. It's our hope and prayer that you and your loved one might be living well in spite of a mental health challenge. Yes, it can happen, even for you and for your loved one.

**One step at a time**

***Prayer:***

*Father, thank You for giving me the courage to pick up this book. I pray for continued courage to face the hard things that I need to learn, and do, in loving a person with a mental health diagnosis.*

*Forgive me for putting blame on my loved one for their behavior, as if they can willingly control the chemistry of their brain. Keep me mindful that they are just as upset with this 'disruption'. Give me the mind of Christ, that I may be compassionate, empathetic, and wise. Most of all, please grant me the ability to be encouraging and supportive as we travel this journey together.*

*In Jesus' name. Amen.*

# Chapter 2

# Can My Loved One Recover?

*Mental Health Recovery: A Hope and a Future*

Some folks will tell you that there is no such thing as mental health recovery. They view mental health issues, such as bipolar disorder or schizoaffective disorder, to be lifelong illnesses that people have to learn how to live with or live in spite of. Now that's an interesting concept, because in one respect they are correct. Many of the diagnoses that someone would receive from a mental health issue would be things that you're going to have your entire life. For instance, Brad has bipolar. He will have it when he dies, but as he says, "I will not die from it."

There's an interesting faction of people that have a mental health diagnosis who perceive themselves as being permanent victims of their mental health challenge. We, in Fresh Hope, look at it differently, as does SAMHSA (Substance Abuse and Mental Health Services Administration, the federal branch of the mental health recovery. They see it more as we do, that recovery is possible. They define recovery as 'A process of change through which individuals improve their health and wellness, live a self-directed life, and strive to reach their full potential.'

Now, we want to be clear and define what recovery exactly is. First of all, recovery is an individual journey. It's not a sprint, but it's a marathon – and it looks different for everyone. While there is no simple direct line and linear way to go through to the point of recovery, there are certainly principles as we have in our Fresh Hope tenets that help move people through recovery. You might say it's a little bit like grief work, because working through grief is not linear or ordered. All recovery journeys include similar aspects, but each journey is different. No two individuals go through it in the same way. That's true for mental health recovery as well.

It's important to note that there are no easy answers, but there *are* answers and that's part of the journey to living well in spite of having a mental health diagnosis. By the way, that's how we like to look at it from a Fresh Hope perspective, that it is quite possible for people to live well *in spite of* having a mental health diagnosis. Now, living well will look different for different people, but it is feasible to be more than just coping, trying to survive life. You *can* have more than that. SAMHSA has a definition of mental health recovery that we find very helpful: "Recovery is a process of change through which individuals improve their health and wellness, live a self-directed life, and strive to reach their full potential." (samhsa.gov)

> **"Living well in spite of"**

Through the Recovery Support Strategic Initiative, SAMHSA has delineated four major dimensions that support a life in recovery (samhsa.gov/find-help/recovery):

- Health
- Home
- Purpose
- Community

SAMHSA cites ten marks of recovery. The first one is hope. Imagine that–hope is the foundation of recovery. Person-driven is the second. Third, recovery may take many paths. The fourth mark of recovery is that it is holistic. Peer support is involved. It's relational; it's cultural; it addresses trauma. Number nine, that every person brings unique strengths and responsibilities to their own recovery; and number 10, that respect is always given.

The belief that recovery is real provides the essential and motivating message of a better future; that people can and do overcome the internal and external challenges, barriers, and obstacles that confront them. Being the initial catalyst of the recovery process, I believe that it's not only fostered by peers, families, providers, allies, and others, but also by faith. With the faith of Romans 8:28, God can take all things and make them work out together for our good.

When that faith is added to internalized hope, that life can be better, that there can be a future, now we have a phenomenally strong hope. One important thing to do is to nurture your loved one in understanding that you believe they've got a great future; that you believe there's a way through this to a new day. Assure them that things won't always stay this way, and that there is hope and healing ahead.

Hopelessness comes about when you feel that you've lost your future. So if someone has a life-altering diagnosis – physical, emotional, or mental – and it alters their desired future, it is going to bring about some hopelessness. But starting to internalize hope is a process of coming to terms with the fact that in spite of it not being the future they want, there is, in fact, a future. And it can be a good future, possibly even better than what they planned.

You may notice that we use the phrase 'living well in spite of'. This is because many people get tripped up on the word 'recovery', interpreting it to mean that the condition is eradicated. Since we learn to *manage* our mental health challenge and can never be rid of it, we follow SAMSHA's working definition of recovery:

> A process of change through which individuals improve their health and wellness, live a self-directed life, and strive to reach their full potential.

Can your loved one really recover? The answer is, yes. They do recover in the sense of that they improve their health and wellness, they live a self-directed life, and they can strive to reach their full potential. How that looks is different for everybody, but it can be done.

One determining factor in recovery is attitude, both of your loved one and everyone around them. It's interesting to note the death rate of people with different types and stages of cancer. Numerous studies show that the stage of cancer doesn't predict the time of death. Sometimes people in Stage 2 die, while a person diagnosed when in Stage 4 of the same cancer lives. Who knows why that happens? We believe that some of that can be attributed to attitude. Doctors will tell you that for any of our physiological issues, attitude matters in recovery. The same is true with mental health issues. Your attitude – your belief that things can be better, that they have potential, that this is not over, that there's an answer for it – can really make a difference for your loved one and for you.

Do as much as you can to keep your loved one from believing that this is some kind of life sentence and this is all they are going to get out of life. I think of the scene in *As Good As It Gets*, where Jack Nicholson asked, "What if this is as good as it gets?" The truth is, that if a person believes they can't recover, they won't.

In research conducted by Dr. Shane Lopez on hope, he proves that it is clinically possible that hope is catching, and that you can borrow hope from someone. This tells us that you can 'loan' hope to your loved one in your attitude and belief that they can have a future, and they can have their life back.

# Three Phases to Living Well in Spite of a Mental Health Disorder/Diagnosis

**THRIVING**

**COPING**

**SURVIVING**

1. Choosing to Live     2. Learning to Live     3. Living Well

Living Well does not mean that you no longer have a mental health disorder, but, it does mean that the disorder no longer rules or interrupts your life. It means that you proactively manage your disorder so that you might flourish to your fullest potential life.

Copyright 2016 Fresh Hope for Mental Health

When people are in that first phase of **surviving**, they're merely attempting to choose to live. They may have just been diagnosed, or it might be after an episode and they've just gotten out of the hospital, but regardless, their life has been totally interrupted. They've just gotten stable after that hospitalization or that episode. The key decision that they have to make at this point is that they want to move forward, that they want to get up and they want to choose to live. They want their life back. They're going to begin to learn new tools, coping mechanisms if you will, and that's when they start moving to phase two.

Phase two is the **coping** phase. It's where they're learning how to live again. They're learning how to take back their life with the knowledge that they have a mental health disorder and that they have an issue. So following that decision to choose to live, they begin to get back up and cope with everyday life, learning skills to empower them to live well in spite of their mental health challenge. This is the phase of filling their toolbox with new skills, a new way of thinking and living.

The illness is still there. A lot of thought, a lot of care, a lot of every day is going to be spent on simply getting up in the morning. It's going to be somewhere around 50/50, where your loved one will be spending about 50% of their time working at getting up and learning and working the tools. and 50% of getting up but falling back. It probably won't be a steady incline of progress, but will be a zig-zag of ups and downs. But if they are working the tools, they will improve and start living. This is the phase where you start encouraging small activities, like going for a walk or out to a movie or for ice cream. They might even start going back to work in this phase.

Be prepared that the phases have no set time limit. Some people are in a phase for months, while some stay in the same phase for years.

Another thing to understand is that in certain aspects of your loved one's life, they may be in the third phase, but in another area of their life, they may be only in phase two. It's complex, and varies a lot. Resist the tendency to want to tell your loved one, 'This is the phase you should be in by now', or 'This is what you need to do'.

The third phase, **thriving,** is where people are living well, where they've taken back their lives. They're living a full and rich life in spite of the mental health disorder by proactively using the tools and skills that they've developed in their toolbox. For instance, Brad has been living well since 2002. He has had no major episodes or disruption of life. Living well does not mean that your loved one no longer has a mental health disorder, but it does mean that the disorder no longer rules or is interrupting your daily lives. Thriving means that your loved one proactively manages their disorder so that they might flourish to their fullest potential.

Let's talk about your role in your loved one's recovery for a bit. Research shows that when someone has supportive family and friends, they have a greater chance of realizing the best possible outcome for their recovery.

**It takes a team of people**

It takes a team of people. It's not just a good doctor, it's not just a good therapist, but it's loved ones and a community of people that support them. You are key in creating that environment for your loved one, for them to desire to want to take back their life.

(Donna) With his manic episode in 1995, I felt very protective of Brad. I wasn't mad at him. I was more angry at how people were or were not acting toward him. Seven years later, he relapsed. Brad had taken a double dosage of his meds, so he decided to skip the next day. But his mind was already racing and convinced him he didn't need to be medicated. By the time the incident happened, he had been off his meds for two weeks.

I was so mad at Brad that he had messed up his meds. If he had just used the pill organizers that I had asked him over and over to use, he would have known he had already taken his medicine. And then he assumed the next day he knew how to solve the problem. Church members who had stood by us the first time, not believing the claims, now left. When it happened the second time, they were done. We lost half of the congregation, and had to take a 50% pay cut. We lost our home as a result, and had to move to an apartment. That had been our dream home, but it had brought only pain and sadness while we lived in it.

A close pastor friend sat me down and asked, 'Are you willing to do this again?" After some thought, I was able to respond, 'I am. But I'm really angry.' Brad was terrified I was going to leave him. Even through my anger at him putting us in this situation – again – I knew I was committed to stay. But I adamantly proclaimed, "But I will be gone if this happens again. I can't go through it a third time."

If you support or enable them too much, they won't do well. If you don't encourage or support them enough, they won't do well. It's a delicate balance of just the right amount. If you're totally hands-off and you don't help them at all, then they may not recover. There are many people who simply could not get back up and stay up in their mental health recovery because they had no one there for them in day-to-day living. They had no family or friends to help them figure out how to live well in spite of the mental health challenge they were facing.

Your role is one of balance. It's a difficult balance, like a teeter-totter, of being just enough and not too little. That's why we advocate for the importance of a support system of those who have been there for you, maybe through a support group, and friends and family. Brad tells people with a diagnosis over and over that they need the support of other people. They can't do it by themselves.

*A bit of reflection:*

Do you believe your loved one can recover? What are some things you have said or done to assure them you of your support?

_____

_____

_____

_____

What phase(s) and in what aspects would you say your loved one is in at this time?

_____

_____

_____

## What Does Wellness Look Like?

What does wellness look like when someone has a mental illness? That's a really good question. First of all, you have to understand that when someone has been diagnosed with a mental health diagnosis such as depression or schizoaffective disorder or bipolar, they're not necessarily going to be constantly sick. With bipolar disorder, there may be episodes; but there also may be weeks, seasons, and even long periods of time with no symptoms or problems. Now, once someone is on medicine and those are the right medicines, they shouldn't display many symptoms at all. The reason medicine is given is to help take away the symptoms.

I (Brad) believe there are key factors for people who have a mental illness to achieve wellness; key signs that they're beginning to live well, that they're beginning to really live a fulfilling life instead of life being sucked out of them by their mental health disorder.

The **first** thing is having the right doctor. It's key. Your loved one has to have a doctor that they trust, that they connect with, where they feel heard. It's important that the doctor responds to what your loved one is saying, instead of just telling them what they need to do and what they need to think. I always tell people, "If you feel like your doctor's not listening to you and doesn't respect what you're saying, then you need to find a different doctor." That's how important it is to your loved one's recovery to have the right doctor.

**Secondly**, your loved one needs talk therapy. This counselor is another key person that your loved one must have a good relationship with and can trust. Wellness also requires taking the right medicine. Sometimes that requires some trial and error until the best combination is found. And as stated earlier, having the right attitude is essential. Your loved one needs a right attitude of saying, "I can do this. I can recover. It may be hard work, but I can recover."

One of the best symptoms of living well is when you see your loved one attempting to get their life back and they're beginning to again do things they love. They are contributing to their family, and beginning to contribute to the community around them.

Probably the first step of beginning to live well is when your loved one hits rock bottom due to their mental health issue. **When they decide that the pain of getting better is less than the pain of staying sick, that's the sign that your loved one truly wants to learn how to live well.**

I (Brad) feel strongly that what helped me get better was the fact that I had an accountability team consisting of my wife, my doctor, and a team of trusted peers. The team had access to my doctor, who had access to his wife. Donna had access to both the accountability group and to the doctor. Everyone could talk to each other, and I was being held accountable for every aspect in my life. That was great motivation for me to get well, and I strongly recommend to everyone with a mental health diagnosis to be sure and set up their own accountability team, and give permission for them all to speak to each other.

> **When they decide that the pain of getting better is less than the pain of staying sick, that's the sign that your loved one truly wants to learn how to live well**

Living well will look differently for everyone. It won't look the same for even those who have the same diagnosis. The brain with bipolar in a 30-year-old is going to be different than in a 60-year-old. Depression will look different in a teen than it does in a 50-year-old. And even living well is going to look different between individuals.

It's also important to note that your loved one's degree of living well will have a lot to do with how they see their life as fulfilling and meaningful. And sometimes living well is greatly affected and changed because the disease may have gotten so bad or has been chronic for so long. But the important thing to remember is that your loved one *can* live well. They don't have to live sick. They don't have to live with symptoms 24/7. The symptoms can be minimized, and in many cases taken away, so to speak, so that your loved one can go on with their life.

Hanging out with others who are living well is another sign of someone living well. Why? Because we become like those we hang around with. If you have ever parented a teen, you know exactly what we mean. As a parent of a teen, you become especially concerned about who your teen spends time with since their behavior and attitude will be greatly affected by those peers!

And so it is with those of us who have a mental health challenge. If we hang out with people who are not living well, we won't develop the skills for living well since we won't see it modeled in those peers (others who have a diagnosis). But put someone with a diagnosis with peers/friends who are living well in spite of their mental health challenges and we are likely to begin living well ourselves. In many respects, one could say that mental illness is caught. Of course you can't 'catch' a mental illness from someone who has a mental illness, just like you can't catch cancer from someone. But the positive attitude of one cancer patient can begin to be 'catching' for a fellow cancer patient. And it is the same with a mental illness. The attitude of those who have a challenge and what they believe about the process of recovery will be catching to your loved one.

## Your Relationship with Their Doctor

One of the things that we believe strongly and that worked for us as a husband and wife with Brad having a diagnosis and Donna being the loved one, is how important that Donna had access to Brad's doctor. We truly believe that you as a loved one need to have access to the doctor. The more correct information the doctor and therapist have, the better the doctor can help your loved one, as well as you. We encourage all the members of Fresh Hope Groups to give access of their loved ones to their doctor. When you're trying to help your loved one and you have access to their doctor, your loved one will have accountability, and the doctor is going to have a lot more information to be better equipped to help your loved one.

You've probably experienced this: your loved one hasn't been doing well, but on the particular day of their doctor's appointment, they feel better and aren't remembering how bad it's been for the last three weeks. But by having you there as a loved one, it helps them remember. Donna went with Brad to his appointments for quite some time until Brad was at a point of stability and owning his own recovery. On top of that, Brad had an accountability group for almost 10 years following his relapse, in which he had to answer to guys that were his peers in ministry. It was that circle of accountability that really helped him get better.

Maybe you're the parent of a young adult who wants to return home to live due to their mental health circumstances, but who has not given you access to their doctor. You may want to leverage that in order to help them. For instance, you might say, "You're welcome to live here, and we will help in any way we can. But you're going to have to give us access to the doctor, or you can't live here."

## Devotional Reflection

*A bit of reflection:*

What are two key factors for people who have a mental illness to achieve wellness?

___

___

___

___

What does Pastor Brad say is the catalyst to a person starting a journey to recovery?

_____

_____

_____

Why is it important for you to have access to your loved one's doctor?

_____

_____

_____

Take a moment to write Romans 8:28 below, emphasizing the words 'know' and 'good'. Then reflect how this passage encourages you.

_____

_____

_____

***Prayer:***

*Father, thank You for leading me to this book. I know there are no easy answers to our situation, but I am grateful for the available resources to help us, especially Fresh Hope. Help me to remember that recovery is a marathon, not a sprint, and that my loved one's recovery will be unique.*

*Forgive me when my feelings of hopelessness overtake my hope in You and in the process. Give me strength and wisdom to help guide my loved one from surviving to coping and finally, to live a thriving life. Help me to balance my efforts to be encouraging, yet not enabling, as together we journey to recovery.*

*In Jesus' name. Amen.*

# Chapter 3

# Believe It or Not: There Is Hope

*When the Feelings of Hopelessness Overshadow the Reality of Hope*

Chances are that you are worried sick, worn out, and wanting answers. We understand. Chances are that you are beginning to wonder if life will ever return to "normal" again. We understand. You're scared. You are so worn out. And you have more questions than answers. We understand. And while you have been desperately holding on to hope as tightly as possible, hopelessness has begun to set in to the unspoken part of your soul. We understand. Why? Because we have experienced it. We have been there. And there is a way forward. Believe it or not, there is hope.

Sometimes in this life we earn 'degrees' that we didn't sign up for at a university. The two of us (Donna and Brad) feel as though we have earned life-living Doctorates in the field of mental illness. Each of us grew up with a parent who had bipolar disorder. We were loved ones early in life, but had no idea. We also had no idea when we married that we shared this commonality. It was 'back then', when you didn't talk about those things. But sooner or later 'those things' get to the point where you have to talk about them.

Mental illness didn't stop at our parents' generation. Brad's diagnosis came in 1995 after a very public manic episode that shook our lives to the core. This threw

Donna into a situational bout of depression while trying to stay sane and be the rock of the family, dealing with all the pain, brokenness, and desperation that mental illness had brought into our lives. Unfortunately, it did not stop with our generation either.

(Donna) I've lived through the depths of hopelessness to find the true hope in Christ. For months prior to Brad's manic episode, I knew my husband was not doing well. He had become a different man than I had married 14 years earlier. He totally consumed himself with all that was involved with a church relocation. I asked for a meeting with the other pastors and told them outright, 'Something is wrong. Brad needs help'. They agreed that he was difficult to work with, but no one acknowledged anything more, and nothing was done to help him. To me, the leadership was more concerned about the growth of the church than about my husband. That's what really hurt.

On top of Brad being completely immersed in relocating our church to a former manufacturing plant, the week before the incident, he was part of a group of pastors traveling to churches on behalf of our church body about contemporary worship. The other pastors were in complete opposition to Brad's views, and made personal attacks on Brad as well as during the presentations. To make it even worse, they were confined in a van for days traveling between churches. It was a horrible experience where Brad was put in extremely high-stress situations. His manic incident occurred two nights after he returned home. I believe the harsh reactions he endured that week were another catalyst to trigger the episode. Just as stress triggers behaviors in any of us, I want you to realize that any level of stress will greatly intensify a mental health issue.

**Any level of stress will greatly intensify a mental health issue**

After the manic episode, we hit bottom. And in hindsight, how people reacted is what caused hopelessness, more so than what actually happened. We were smeared in the news, received condemning letters from pastors across the country, and many friendships ceased. No one acknowledged mental illness as even a possibility – instead, that it was all Brad's sinfulness. Because Brad was not allowed to plead 'no contest' by the church body, we had a horrible experience in court. The lawyer did a poor job, and despite conflicting witness accounts, the judge delivered a guilty verdict. We appealed with a new lawyer, and the decision was reversed. But the church encouraged Brad to resign.

Brad and I knew we needed help, but no one seemed to care. When we asked the church elders to cover the expenses for an outpatient hospital that would help us both, they declined. I felt absolute despair and hopelessness, and wept inconsolably. But seeing how upset I was, they reconsidered.

Here is also why it is so important to get your loved one to be seen – immediately – by a psychiatrist; not a Primary Care Physician. Shortly after Brad's manic episode, a medical doctor had given Prozac to Brad. No one knew Brad had bipolar, including Brad. Now we know that anti-depressants taken without a mood stabilizer send people with bipolar into mania. By the time we reached the hospital, Brad's thoughts were spinning so fast that he felt he could run it! The doctor recognized immediately that Brad had bipolar disorder. After a few days, when he asked why it took so long to tell him, she responded, 'Because you wouldn't shut up long enough for me to talk!' Taking the wrong medicine can make your loved one worse. That's why it's **so important for people to be seen by psychiatrist.**

My hopelessness continued throughout that summer, and at the hospital. Sitting in group and individual counseling sessions was extremely difficult. It made me so sad, and I even got hives. The stress was also showing up in stomach issues. I lost 20 pounds that summer. It didn't matter what I ate, or if I didn't eat at all.

I ended up in the emergency room because the pain was so bad. I also felt great anger. I would go into the bathroom and just scream into the towels after Brad was asleep. It was scary anger, and I had never before felt anger so strongly. [One person later described me as being so angry that I even was 'a little scary'!] We were traumatized. I was in fight mode, and I was fighting for my husband.

I returned home after a week, with a bud of hope starting to grow. At the end of Brad's stay, the hospital gave a Plan of Restoration to the church leadership, for Brad to return to the church and process mental illness with them. After listening to the medical staff, they finally understood this was not a sin issue, but was a medical issue. But sadly, the Plan was not followed, and Brad was not allowed to return to the church.

We're now able to see the pressures and stress of moving the church were the trigger for Brad's bipolar. Most often, that's the case. Some event or succession of events triggers the mental health situation. If I were to identify how I first started seeing Brad's behavior change, it would be with instances of extreme anger. The kids were the brunt of that anger many times. He would get in their faces and not stop until he was satisfied, even after they acknowledged their mistake. Usually by then the kids and I were in tears. Brad couldn't see what he was doing, because his brain was sick.

When behavior doesn't make sense in loved one, it's probably mental health issue. That's why it's called *behavioral health*.

## *A bit of reflection:*

How do you relate with Donna? Has your world been tilted on its axis by a loved one's actions?

_____

_____

_____

_____

What extreme behaviors have you observed with your loved one? Are you able to identify triggers for those behaviors?

_____

_____

_____

_____

Donna knew that something was not right with Brad, and went to the church leadership for help. Have your cries for help gone unheeded? Who else might you be able to reach out to?

_____

_____

_____

_____

You and your loved one must be proactive in seeking the right doctors and treatment. Seek out recommendations. Do internet searches for service providers in your community. What steps have you taken / are taking in these areas?

_____

_____

_____

_____

**So when we say, "We understand," we really do. And we are here to tell you that there you are not alone. And while we respect that each of us has a different journey, there is a way forward. There is a future. No matter what. The tears you have cried for your loved one have been heard by the King of the Universe as liquid prayers. There is hope!**

We can tell you that today, our lives are good. We got through some pretty awful storms through the years, but not without some scars. And yes, it was painful!

But those scars are proof of the Lord's faithfulness. Even the pain has been and is being redeemed. We are still learning how to weather the storms of life, because we know that there will be other storms. That's just life.

**You are NOT alone. There is healing. There is hope.**

Max Lucado is one of our favorite authors. In his book *You'll Get Through This* (©2013 Thomas Nelson) is a 'mantra' that fits any and all difficult times we might go through:

> *You'll get through this.*
>
> *It won't be painless.*
>
> *It won't be quick.*
>
> *But God will use this mess for good.*
>
> *Don't be foolish or naïve.*
>
> *But don't despair either.*
>
> *With God's help, you'll get through this.*

This little mantra is realistic. It doesn't ignore the pain, but it also doesn't leave out what the Lord can do through the difficulties of life.

Chances are that you have felt hopeful at times regarding your loved one's recovery. There's also a pretty good chance that you have a nagging fear in the pit of your belly, wondering if things will ever get better. You most likely are grieving and are suffering from heart wounds. And you maybe have some of your own issues on top of everything else. You may feel you're being pulled down into a deep dark hole of despair yourself. Or you may be giving so much to your loved one that you feel like the life is being sucked right out of you.

We are living proof that there is hope – true, realistic hope. We're not talking about the wishful-thinking type of hope. That's where you don't know what the outcome will be, and you just hope it is good. We're talking about the real hope that is firmly fixed in Romans 8:28. Real hope that God can do all things and work all things out together for good for those who love Him and are called according to His plan and His purpose. That's the only real and living hope that can help you in spite of the hopelessness you feel.

We understand that the feelings of hopelessness are very real. Actually, hope isn't necessarily a feeling at all. It's more of a choice to believe that the Lord will work all things out together for your good. In contrast, hopelessness is a feeling based on something that's not necessarily true.

But what we can't do is pump each other up spiritually, and ignore the hopeless feelings. Feelings have to be felt in order for us to heal and move forward. In fact, if you dismiss the pain and the grief, and simply stuff the feelings down or sugar-coat them with some sort of positive toxicity, that stuffed pain will show up when you least expect it. Think about trying to hold a huge beach ball underwater, out of sight. Despite your best efforts, you inevitably will lose your grip and the ball will pop above surface. It's like that with your feelings of hopelessness. You go along okay for a while, until the pressures get so great that it all rushes to the surface for everyone to see.

The reality is that when mental illness hits a family, it hurts. There's pain: there are problems, difficulties, and frustrations. And the feelings and pain that come from all of these *has* to be owned and processed. But how? By working through them: feeling the feelings, allowing yourself to grieve, and sharing with others and being heard by those who care. Working through the feelings is something that happens when you sit down with others who have gone or are going through the same sorts of things, and you begin to share your story. You express your feelings and let them out: tears, frustrations, fears – everything that encompasses hopelessness.

By acknowledging your feelings of hopelessness and pain, you can begin to process them. Then you can hold on to hope *in spite of* the fact you might not feel hopeful. It's important to understand that hopelessness is rooted in the loss of future. And when your loved one is struggling with a mental illness, that affects everyone around them. It can end up feeling like the future has been lost and you end up feeling extremely hopeless.

Hopelessness comes about when the present and the future seem interrupted, and in some cases, the future seems destroyed. The feelings of hopelessness are certainly real, but for those of us who are Christians, there is never a hopeless situation.

There's a lot of grief that everyone has to work through when mental illness shows up in a family, within a marriage, or in a friendship. But like we've said, there is also good news. The feelings of hopelessness are real, but for those of us who are in Christ, there is always a future of hope. There is always a way when there seems to be no way. There is always a way through the pain.

Unfortunately, all too often in the Christian church, what happens is that we sugarcoat pain using the hope of Christ. We want to alleviate the pain because we honestly don't know what to do with it. We sugarcoat their pain and encourage them to get past their feelings. And yet the reality is, pain has to be dealt with in working towards wellness.

Lest you feel like we're going to try to cheer you up with positive toxicity by sugarcoating your pain, we are not. In fact, we encourage you to feel the pain, to cry, to process and work through what you are feeling. You can't heal without feeling. It's normal to have the emotions. So go ahead and grieve, but grieve as those who have hope.

Somewhere we've gotten this mistaken idea that we can just 'pull ourselves up by our bootstraps' and miraculously find more faith to get through anything. Well, that perspective is not really faith. Faith is when you're feeling those horrible emotions and living a situation, but you know that the Lord will bring you through it in spite of how awful it feels.

We need to feel and process our pain and our difficulties, and then choose to put our hope in God. We need to learn how to lament, how to pour out our pain and complain to God, and yet choose to believe in Him. The Old Testament contains many laments. Most of the Book of Psalms are laments, and of course the Book of Lamentations itself. There's something to be learned about how to go through life's difficulties by learning how to do godly laments. You'll have the opportunity to do that as you go through this book.

**There *is* a new way to a new future**

There *is* a new way to a new future. It may not be the future you thought it would be, but it's a good future. So this book and the Principles of Recovery are about healing by recognizing, feeling, and then choosing. We feel the hopelessness not by pretending it's not there, but rather by processing it; not sugarcoating it, but by cleaning out the wound.

These seven principles of recovery are core beliefs that are, for the most part, universally true of those of us who have loved and are loved ones of those who have a mental health diagnosis. We each face the challenges in our own way, but if we love someone with a mental illness, we will face challenges. The Principles of Recovery are at the core of working through towards living well.

As we do that, we choose hope by faith. Hope doesn't take away or wipe out our feelings, but we choose to put our hope in the Lord Himself, who is the anchor of the storms we go through.

We don't normally think about moving towards an anchor during a storm, but during the storms of life, that's when you have to hold onto hope and pull closer and closer to the Lord. Paul talks about us having this hope as an anchor, and that's the kind of hope we're talking about in this book.

If you're a boating enthusiast, you might be familiar with the nautical concept of kedging. Kedging a ship or a boat means to actually drop an anchor onto a rock in preparation for a storm. The intent is to catch the anchor in a cleft of a large rock. Then you put out to open waters to protect your boat by keeping the line taut so it holds to that rock throughout the storm. And in fact, you actually pull just a little bit closer to that rock during a storm to keep the anchor caught in the cleft. Keeping the line tight keeps you anchored to the rock, and protects the ship.

In this book, our goal is to help you deal with all these things as you walk this road with your loved one who is suffering from a mental illness. We want to help and guide you through a process where your hopelessness is felt and heard, but at the same time you are able to hold on to hope. And first things first, you need to understand: you can't do this alone.

## *A bit of reflection:*

Holding onto hope, kedging your ship during a storm can be more than exhausting. How exhausted are you? Have you had days like Donna, sitting in the backyard and crying out to God?

_____

_____

_____

_____

What are the issues that cause the most concern about the future?

_____

_____

_____

_____

Do you at times feel more hopeless than hopeful about the future? How empty is your hope tank? *(It's important to be honest about this. That's how you process the pain.)*

_____

_____

_____

_____

Are you afraid to allow yourself to feel the pain, frustrations, and difficulties out of fear that if you do, you won't be able to be hopeful and strong for your loved one? How can the words of 1 Corinthians 10:13 encourage you?

*No trial has overtaken you that is not faced by others. And God is faithful: He will not let you be tried beyond what you are able to bear, but with the trial will also provide a way out so that you may be able to endure it.*

_____

_____

_____

In your own words, explain what it means to process the feelings of hopelessness, and choose hope at the same time.

_____

_____

_____

_____

## Devotional Reflection

Take time to read carefully Psalm 13. This Psalm is a lament. A lament is a passionate expression of grief or sorrow. In this case, someone is pouring out their hurts, pains, and frustrations out to the Lord. They cry out in desperation. It's a prayer, a cry for help reminding the Lord that He alone is the one Who can solve their solution. And at the end of almost every lamentation in the Bible (with some exceptions), the one crying closes the lament by telling the Lord that they will wait for Him to move, to solve the issue. They close by choosing to place their trust and help in the Lord. They choose to believe and trust in spite of their pain and storm that they are weathering.

The lament serves as a wonderful example of what it means to process and feel our pain, and at the same time to choose hope. The Bible shows us over and over that it is OK to feel and to express those feelings to the Lord. But the Bible doesn't teach us only to vent our feelings to the Lord. We then need that final step: to choose to hold onto His hope, anchored, kedged to the Rock of our Salvation. So, we vent, but then we choose to focus on Him, not the problems. We choose to trust Him in the midst of the problems.

(Interestingly enough, research shows that when people only vent about their problems, they get sicker. Yet we also know that when people don't deal with their pain, the pain begins to deal with them. Scripture teaches us to vent and to process the pain, but not to keep looping the problems over and over in our thinking and then becomes negative ruminating. By the Scriptures teaching us to end a lament with statements of faith and trust, it actually loops our thinking out of lamenting and instead focuses us on the Lord instead. It's amazing how science is catching up with the Bible!)

We encourage you to write your own lament. Take time to do it. Pour your heart out to the Lord. Cry out to Him, complain to Him, tell Him what you need that only He can do as you come face to face with the mental illness of your loved one. Don't be afraid to feel. And when you feel that you have poured everything out that you need to pour out to Him, then close with statements of faith and trust and holding to His hope.

_____

_____

_____

_____

_____

_____

_____

*Believe It or Not: There Is Hope*

*(If you're doing this book within a group of peers, we encourage you to share these laments with one another when you next meet.)*

# Chapter 4

# You Can't Do This Alone

*So Don't Try to Do It Alone!*

When you share your joy with a friend, it multiplies the joy. When you share your burdens with a friend, it divides the load.

Everybody loved Kevin. He was the all-around jock, a wholesome guy. When Jenny and Kevin got married it seemed as they were living a carefree and happy life together. They seemed to have it all. Kevin farmed with his Dad. Because Jenny's family lived in another state, Kevin's parents became like they were her own parents. Times were good. Plenty of money to be made in farming. Along the way Kevin and Jenny were blessed with children. Life was good.

Then came the farm crisis. Now instead of money to be made farming, it seemed as though there was only money to be lost because of farming. It was really the first time Kevin had faced difficulties, and the stress was taking its personal toll on Kevin. Unbeknownst to his family, he started drinking in order to cope with the anxiety attacks. But the drinking alone didn't keep the anxiety at bay. It was only getting worse. And when Kevin confided about it with a buddy, his buddy suggested he try a little pot to take the edge off of the anxiety. It seemed to help for a while. What Kevin didn't know was that he was self-medicating a developing mental health issue, and the self-medication of the pot was about to make things worse. Within months of using the pot he began to hear voices. About a year later, it was apparent to his wife and parents that something was very wrong. Kevin was no longer functioning at all. They got him to a doctor, and he was diagnosed with psycho-affective disorder. The medicine worked. But Kevin refused to take his medicine about half the time because he believed that the meds were going to kill him (due to the paranoia). He wouldn't stop drinking. Wouldn't attend a support group. Wouldn't see a therapist, and sometimes wouldn't even go into see his doctor.

Now, he sits in a rocking chair on the front porch of his parents' farmhouse, smoking cigarettes from sun-up to sun-down. Kevin stares out at the land he used to farm, speaking out loud to the voices he is hearing in his head. Jenny can't take much more and is planning to leave him for the sake of the kids. Kevin seems unwilling, unable to choose to grab ahold of his own recovery. His parents are hopeless...as is his wife. They feel isolated and alone, hopeless and helpless. They can't make him recover, and they aren't doing well themselves.

All alone in a small town in the Midwest where there is so much stigma, what do they do? Where do they go? Who can they talk with who will understand? When Kevin's Dad had open-heart surgery, neighbors and church members called, visited, sent cards, and brought over all kinds of food. And now, those same people who had reached out with such compassion, who know everything going on with Kevin, are nowhere to be seen. No one is calling; there are no visits, no cards, and no casseroles. There is just dead silence. And the silence is killing Kevin's family one breath at a time.

Mental illness is often termed the 'no casserole' illness. This is so true. Through the years we have come to know too many stories about families who never hear from friends, neighbors, or even their church when there is a mental health issue. It's not necessarily because people don't care. More times than not, it is because they don't know what to say. And so the loved ones, as well as the one with the mental health challenge, become even more isolated. And isolation is the petri dish for hopelessness and helplessness. And please note, the isolation that we are talking about is due to not talking about the issues and challenges with others that you are facing as a caregiver. You can be around a lot of people and interact with them daily, and still be isolated. If you don't process what is happening in your family and to your loved one, that part of your life becomes isolated and a breeding ground for your hopelessness and helplessness.

## *A bit of reflection:*

How can you identify with Kevin's wife?

_____

_____

_____

_____


How can you identify with Kevin's parents?

_____

_____

_____

_____

What do Kevin's parents and his wife need?

_____

_____

_____

_____

Where are you on a scale of hopelessness to hope, with 1 being the most hopeless and 10 being filled with hope? Using the same scale, where are you on the scale of helplessness?

_____

_____

_____

_____

∽

(Donna) At the time of Brad's first episode, our kids were only 6th and 2nd graders – in a Christian school. But their classmates were mean to them, and I'm sure it was a result of what their parents had told them. Our kids were very much judged, and treated as if they had done something wrong. They were crushed. Only one teacher brought a meal. Our daughter couldn't understand why her friends' parents wouldn't let them come over to play. She could go to their houses, but they couldn't come to hers. What 7-year-old understands that? All she knew was that she wasn't being treated fairly. I didn't tell Brad a lot of how people treated the kids and me. It would only cause more pain and guilt for him, and of course I didn't want to do that.

The week after Brad had to go before the congregation to apologize, I went to choir practice. I so needed support and reassurance, and I believed that of all places I would be received here with compassion and understanding. Instead, I was shunned. No one talked to me, no one sat by me, and not one gesture of compassion was given. That hurt so deeply.

*A bit of reflection:*

What is the hardest part for you of your loved one's struggle with mental illness?

___

___

___

___

What undeserved judgment and imposed shame have you endured?

___

___

___

___

It is fair to say that isolation, the non-interaction with others about the issues you face as one who loves someone with a mental illness, can potentially cause you to have mental health challenges, too. Studies have shown that isolation actually inhibits our brains from being able to problem solve due to the loss of the neuroplasticity of the brain (*Use It Or Lose It: How Neurogenesis Keeps The Brain Fit For Learning*, ncbi.nlm.nih.gov/pmc/articles). So it is imperative for you as one who loves someone with a mental health issue to find others to talk and interact with who have been through what you are going through. You cannot do this alone. The help and care of others who have walked and are walking through the same things is imperative to your own mental health.

**Thus, our first Fresh Hope Principle for those who are loved ones is:**

*My loved one's mental health challenge has also left me feeling helpless and hopeless. Therefore, I choose the help of others in learning about the disorder and choosing healthy boundaries for myself.*

Simply put, you cannot do this alone.

If you have walked alongside your loved one struggling with their mental health for any length of time, you have most likely found yourself feeling helpless, frustrated, confused, and alone. And if the road has been very rocky at all, you most likely have felt hopeless at times. Worry not, it's normal. What you are feeling and experiencing is quite normal for those who are loved ones. Even if you have found the listening ear of a friend or two, there is still nothing like talking with others who have "been through it" and have insights and hope to offer. Having the support and insights of those who have gone through the same things is key to staying emotionally healthy.

> **You cannot do this alone**

So the first step to being an emotionally healthy caregiver of a mentally challenged person is to choose the help of others by connecting with them. Here are a few suggestions:

- Seek out those you know who have walked through what you are walking through and ask to meet with them on a regular basis.

- Connect through a support group such as Fresh Hope or any local mental health support group. If you can't find a group in your area, consider attending an online Fresh Hope group meeting.

- Connect with a counselor. They can help you see options, and how to stay healthy yourself. But most likely they will not approach this as a peer-helping-a-peer situation. They can share their personal journeys, but their code of ethics will limit the personal depth of your relationship. So, it's not quite the same. You can't call them at any time, and they won't come over when you need someone late at night.

- Connect through a NAMI *Family to Family* class.

**Whatever you do, don't try to do this alone.** You need support and encouragement as the caregiver to your loved one. If you continue to do this all alone without support and care from others who have "been there", you'll end up being of no help to your loved one – or yourself – because you won't be able to give from a point of strength, care, and love.

Just as connecting with others is a choice, isolation is also a choice. One of these two choices will help your loved one and you. The other will only breed more helplessness and more hopelessness. Isn't it a clear choice?

When you connect with others who have or are walking through the same things, you suddenly realize that you are not alone. It is estimated that one out of every five adults in the US has a diagnosable mental health issue in any given year. That means that most likely 25% of the American population is experiencing what you are experiencing. But no one is talking, no one is connecting, when the truth – and the good news –is, you are NOT alone!

In connecting with others, you are also gaining insights about mental health challenges and the various issues involved. In doing so, you can begin to separate the illness/disorder from who your loved one truly is. This is one of the reasons that in our Fresh Hope groups we include both those with a diagnosis and those who are loved ones. We have seen it happen over and over when a loved one hears someone else with a diagnosis share an insight or frustration and it becomes an 'ah-ha' moment for them. And the loved one gains insight about the disorder, now better able to separate the disorder from the one they love who has a mental health diagnosis.

Learning more about your loved one's diagnosis is so important. It will help you separate the diseased brain part from who your loved one is without the brain issues. The more you know, the more you are in an emotionally healthy spot to give support to your loved one. Where do you go to learn about your loved one's diagnosis? One of the best places is in a NAMI 12-week free Family-to-Family class (nami.org/findsupport).

One of the things that has truly amazed us about the Fresh Hope group experience is the collective wisdom and insight within the group participants. The wealth of insights, points of transformation, practical options, and potential solutions is astounding when you have a concentrated group of people who are walking through the same thing in life. Prior to experiencing the years of leading a support group, we didn't understand how powerful a group of peers helping and encouraging one another can truly be. Connecting with others who are experiencing like issues in their journeys can become a key to you gaining transformational insights, strength, courage, and hope for your journey.

Choose to connect with others regarding what you are walking through with your loved one. You will be helping both them and yourself. Chances are if you've made it this far into the book, you are either already part of a group, or plan to join one – or you might even be part of a group that is using this book! You will be amazed at the hope, strength, insights, and compassion to be found through others who have 'been there, done that'.

**Choose to connect with others**

## In Your Own Words

*My loved one's mental health challenge has also left me feeling helpless and hopeless. Therefore, I choose the help of others in learning about the disorder and choosing healthy boundaries for myself.*

Rewrite Principle #1 in your own words, personalizing it for your situation:

_____

_____

_____

_____

## Devotional Reflection

The third part of Recovery Principle #1 is:

Together, we have understanding. We remind each other of the Lord's love, and that He alone can do all things. He is the source of our hope, and in Him we can overcome all things.

***"I can do everything through Him who gives me strength." Philippians 4:13 (NIV)***

There's great comfort in knowing that we are not alone and we don't have to do this journey alone. Together, we do have better understanding. And together we can remind each other of the Lord's love. After all, He – not you – can do all things. We can look to Him as the source of our hope. We *will* get through this and are overcomers in and through Him.

You can do this, because He gives you the strength. If you are weak and fearful, turn to Him. Ask Him to be your strength. Focus on Him, not your circumstances. Spend time with Him so that He can fill you with His sure and certain hope. He loves YOU! He is with YOU! And He is for YOU!

***Prayer:***

*Lord, when I'm hurting and feeling rather hopeless, I so easily isolate myself from others, and instead of reaching out and asking for help, I find myself ruminating and worrying over and over in my mind. Help me, Lord, to speak three simple words. I need help. I cannot do this alone. I need help, help from safe people who have great insight because they have walked this road before me. And of course Lord, more than anything, I need Your help, Your strength, Your courage.*

*I need help in understanding. Help in processing. Help in finding resources. Help in finding the courage and the strength to go through this with my loved one.*

*Help me, Lord, to understand more about the disorder or the dysfunctions of my loved one's brain versus who they are as a person. Help me to separate these two things. Help me to find places of respite. Help me to find places of resources. Help me to find places of refreshment.*

*Lord, bring around me the right people who can speak into my situation and into my life, giving me insights from their own journeys. Keep me open to seeing those people that you have placed around me as gifts from You.*

*In Jesus' name. Amen.*

## Chapter 5

# Relationships Matter

*Being a Healthy You Helps the Relationship*

*"My heart is meant to love you. And so, I will fight for you when you want to give up. Pick you up when you are falling down. And I'll give you my smile when it's hard to find yours. And I will do everything to be the best me I can be and will do all I can to preserve our relationship, so we are at our best as we face this battle together."* (Author Unknown)

Shirley was diagnosed with schizoaffective disorder in the early 1980s. She had suffered many traumatic and life-altering episodes through the years which almost always included psychosis. Many times Shirley's episodes were due to her going off her meds, but sometimes it was merely her brain causing the problems even on the meds. Her husband, Ben, had been by her side through all of it. He was hyper-vigilant and very controlling. After all, he had to be; he never knew when she might go off the 'deep-end' again.

The truth is that Ben becoming so controlling had to do with his unresolved anger over the past and his fears about the future. While he loved Shirley deeply, he believed that she was the only one in the relationship with any problems. Ben felt he had to take care of her as a parent would a disabled child, so much so that when Shirley was doing well and moving forward in her recovery and beginning to take her life back, he became even more controlling out of fear that another episode was coming. He did not see the relationship between them as spouses who were equals, but rather a caregiver for someone who was 'less-than' his equal.

Ben's issues, not only Shirley's, were causing relationship issues that were affecting Shirley's recovery. He was approaching it not as empowering Shirley to take back her life from the disease, but rather his job was to control Shirley and her environment. So when Shirley did begin to truly recover and had several years without any mental health issues, Ben continued to hold her back and not allow her to become his equal. He didn't think he was doing it, but he was.

Shirley's counselor, along with Shirley, attempted to help Ben see where he, too, needed to work through issues. But he failed to see how his unresolved issues were hurting their marriage. He believed he had responded well to Shirley's mental illness. But it was the way was responding that was hurting their relationship. Many of his actions when she was really sick were absolutely necessary. But as she was getting better, his fear created an environment that held Shirley back from living well in spite of her mental health issue. He was not encouraging; he was controlling. Unfortunately, their marriage ended in divorce.

Shirley is doing well today. She is the leader of a recovery group. In spite of having schizoaffective disorder, she is living well. Ben remains angry, hurt, and resentful. After all, how could she reject him after all he had done for her?

## *A bit of reflection:*

If Ben had been willing to look at his issues and work through them, might the outcome of their marriage be different? Why?

_____

_____

_____

Do you believe that Ben might have been holding back Shirley's recovery? How?

_____

_____

_____

How does one deal with the balance of being a caregiver when the one you love is not doing well, vs when they are doing well? How are you doing with this balancing act?

_____

_____

_____

Do you see your loved one as an equal, or do you see your loved one as 'less than' because of their illness?

_____

_____

_____

_____

In what ways have you responded well to your loved one's mental illness? How have you encouraged them in their recovery? In what ways have you not responded well?

_____

_____

_____

_____

What issues can you identify that you need to work through that would be helpful to your relationship?

_____

_____

_____

_____

Through the years of facilitating Fresh Hope support group meetings, we've seen many relationships that are strained or flat-out dysfunctional between the loved ones and those who have a mental health diagnosis, but we are never shocked by it. After all, a mental illness affects how people think and how they act within their relationships. It's the one disease where the infected or diseased organ makes decisions, and so relationships are greatly affected by this issue.

But it's also important as a loved one to remember that you too, have issues. They may not be because of a chemical issue in the brain, but everyone has baggage, emotional issues, so to speak. And because of that you, too, bring difficulties to relationships. For instance, if you just remove the issue of mental illness between you and the person that you care about who has a mental health diagnosis, you're still going to have relationship issues. But put on top of that a mental illness and everything it causes within life itself, it even becomes more important, or it has a more drastic effect upon an already imperfect relationship.

**Thus, our second Fresh Hope Principle for those who are loved ones is:**

*I haven't always responded to my loved one's mental health issue in ways that were good for the relationship. Therefore, I choose to learn better ways to communicate with, support, and encourage my loved one.*

Put simply, your relationship with your loved one who is struggling with their mental health matters. Research shows that when someone with a mental health issue has a caring support system, they do better in recovery (*Taking Good Care of Yourself;* Mental Health America, mhanational.org/taking-good-care-yourself). If you want to be helpful and encouraging to your loved one, it is imperative for you to work on and resolve any issues that you bring to the relationship as well.

You can't look at this as though your loved one is the one with all the issues, that they are the one who is sick. In doing so, you will miss any relationship issues, dysfunctions, and emotional issues that you bring to the relationship. Those who work in the addiction/recovery field of alcoholism will tell you that the one who lives with the alcoholic can be just as sick as the alcoholic. Now, while the effects of a mental illness on a family may not be exactly the same, there is some truth in that statement.

(Donna) After his manic episode, Brad was so fearful of his parents' reactions that he couldn't bring himself to tell them in person. He did have another person tell them. Later that week they came to see us. Here is where his dad's words made a lasting impact, "I don't care what you've done. You're my son and I love you." Brad had waited his entire life to be affirmed by his dad.

Think of it this way: Take the mental illness out of the scenario, and you and your loved one have a relationship. Two equals who bring good things – and also some baggage – to the relationship. This is a universally true fact. So when you put a mental illness on top of this, the relationship is still there but now complicated and exasperated by one person's brain not working properly. This will exhaust, and at times trigger and frustrate the one who loves them. If you as a loved one can acknowledge that you also have issues, and work on them for the sake of your relationship, you will become more helpful in the recovery of your loved one.

**Many diagnoses are episodic**

*Relationships Matter*

One of the challenges of loving someone who has a mental illness is that many diagnoses are episodic. For instance, someone with depression has times where they are clinically depressed and other times when they are not. And within your relationship you go from being a caregiver to being no longer needed in the same way when they are doing well. You are the caregiver, the advocate, and coach, and suddenly when your loved one starts to live well, then you go back to being their spouse, the child, their parent, or friend. Your relationship then changes, based upon the illness. This becomes a relationship challenge.

(Donna) Our own relationship experienced a shift of roles starting with Brad's manic episode. I became Brad's caregiver, protector, advocate, and coach. Though I became a stronger person, it also caused me to become battle weary. I had to take over as the head of the household, in a role I wasn't meant to be in. All of this was going on at the same time I was processing and working through the pain of the situation. As you probably well know, this burden took quite a toll on me.

And then because I was the protector for so long, it has been difficult to return to the roles the way they're supposed to be. I had to rebuild my trust in my husband that had been broken.

It was a number of years before the relationship and roles changed back. This was especially difficult for Brad, as it was important for him to show Donna through his day- to-day living that he didn't need the same kind of care as after the episode. And to be honest, Donna still watches out for Brad's emotional and mental health to this day. She is vigilant in making sure he is doing well. But these shifting of roles and then into a new normal creates issues within the relationships. It takes work, time, and most of all, honesty.

One of the key things we have found in walking through this journey as a couple is the importance of asking questions, as opposed to telling the other what to do. For example, it's human nature to think that when you are saying things like, 'Well, you just need to get more rest and take your medicine," is encouraging someone in their road to recovery. But encouraging someone does not mean that you tell them what they should be doing. This only causes the one you are 'telling' to become defensive. They see it as controlling. Questions instead allow room for interaction and don't take power away from the one who is experiencing mental distress. Questions empower and might encourage them to embrace the solution without needing to get defensive.

We have also learned the importance of giving each other positive observations. For example, I (Donna) will compliment Brad for how he is coping with a specific challenge: "Brad, I've noticed that you seem to be handling the additional stress that's going on right now at the church." It is always more encouraging to look for things your loved one is doing well than to continually point out what is wrong. Admittedly, sometimes finding good can be a little challenging. Sometimes you have to look for the smallest things to be able to point out, but acknowledging even the most basic of tasks (getting up and dressed, brushing their teeth, loading the dishwasher, caring for your pet, vacuuming, putting gas in the car) can have a positive influence on their day.

**Speak the truth in love**

It is also important for you to speak the truth in love. There may be things that are hurting you or that you are concerned about that need to be shared with your loved one. Sharing in truth and love within a setting that is safe for both of you is very important. Otherwise, resentment can easily set in. And when they are well, you'll be left with a whole lot of personal emotional pain and resentment and anger because they got better, and you had to endure all the crap that came your way. What we're trying to say is that if you stuff all of your feelings and frustrations and don't deal with them in truth and love, you'll end up with an oversized bag of resentment afterwards.

As you begin to separate your loved one from their mental illness, it becomes easier to respect and honor them in spite of the illness. This was key to my (Brad's) recovery. Donna never made me feel as though I was 'less than' within our relationship because of my illness. She honored and respected me in spite of it and the pain it caused in our marriage and lives. That does not mean that she excused my behaviors that were hurtful. She held me accountable for them. But she did understand the explanations for the behaviors, that they were part of the illness. This was a key factor for us as a couple. We all need respect and honor. These are key foundations to being in relationship.

There are times when you, as the loved one, can personally benefit from seeing a therapist. It's something you might want to consider. Just as there's no shame in your loved one seeking help for the mental illness, there's also no shame in you seeking help as you go about caregiving. We've met a lot of caregivers/loved ones who have developed a lot of anxiety as they have cared for and loved someone who has a mental illness, and some were becoming quite debilitated by it. After seeing a therapist, they were able to overcome the anxiety before it got to the point of being debilitating. It's important to remember that we all have emotional issues in which we can benefit from some talk therapy. No doubt, you have been triggered by everything you've walked through as a loved one, and you've certainly had feelings and emotions that you've probably shoved down, believing that there isn't time to work on those things 'right now'. But the truth is, if you work through those things when they are happening, they will be less likely to won't build up and cause even more problems down the road. Seeing a therapist or attending a healthy peer support group can make you a better caregiver and loved one.

## In Your Own Words

*I haven't always responded to my loved one's mental health issue in ways that were good for the relationship. Therefore, I choose to learn better ways to communicate with, support, and encourage my loved one.*

Rewrite Principle #2 in your own words, personalizing it for your situation:

_____

_____

_____

_____

## Devotional Reflection

The third part of Recovery Principle #2 is:

> Together, we commit to speaking the truth in love, healing broken relationships and viewing each other as the Lord views us.

**"So let's pursue those things which bring peace and which are good for each other." Romans 14:19 (God's Word Translation, 1995)**

There's great comfort in knowing that the Lord's mercies are new every morning; that mistakes we may have made within our relationship with our loved one can be forgiven, and that we get a fresh start daily. There's great wisdom in just taking it 'one day at a time'. Each day is a fresh new day in the Lord. That is healing for relationships.

It's also great comfort to know how the Lord views you. He sees you through the blood of Jesus as His child as He created you to be. And He sees your loved one the same way. He invites us to daily lay before Him our fears and failures.

You are not perfect. You have and will again make mistakes. Caregiving can bring out the best in us, but it can also reveal many of our shortcomings. By embracing and processing our shortcomings we become more loving, truthful, and caring to the one we love. This is a process. But when we do this, it allows us to grow emotionally and spiritually in spite of being on a difficult journey.

So that resentment, hurt, and anger might not take root in our relationships, we commit ourselves to speaking the truth in love at the appropriate times. It really is truth spoken in love that can also set us free. Remember, truth can be poisonous if given without love, out of anger, or even if spoken at an inappropriate time. Love brings tenderness and discernment as to when and how the truth is shared, thinking of the one receiving it. Love allows speaking the truth to do its work of giving insight, as opposed to causing offense and creating walls instead of removing them. The love of Jesus, along with truth, allows us to truly pursue those things that bring peace and which are really good for each other!

### *Prayer:*

*Lord Jesus, first I want to thank You for my relationship with You. You loved me first. It was Your truth given in love on the cross that set me free and opened the door to my relationship with You. Thank You.*

*Lord, I ask You to show me areas within my relationship with my loved one that I need to address and work on. Sometimes I'm so focused on my loved one and their mental health that I fail to remember that there's a relationship that we have that now is complicated by this illness. So I ask you to give me courage to see where I need to grow and change as a person so that I might become the version of me that You created me to be.*

*Jesus, I lift up my relationship with my loved one to You. I ask You to bless us. By the power of Your Holy Spirit help us to pursue those things that bring peace and which are good for one another. Help each of us to have the courage to speak the truth in love to one another that we, through You, might grow closer to one another. Please bring more laughter, more joy, more hope, and more life into our lives.*

*In Jesus' name. Amen.*

## Chapter 6

# Learn How to Contribute in Appropriate and Healthy Ways

*Some Things Help and Other Things Don't Help:
Knowing the Difference is Key*

Jenna's mom, Linda, was the strong one. She knew Jenna needed to own her own recovery. She couldn't do it for Jenna. After all, Jenna was now 21 and considered an adult, but she sure didn't act like one. Jenna had been diagnosed with a personality disorder at the age of 10. Life was difficult for Jenna, and her inability or unwillingness to do what she needed to do to get better made life difficult for her and everyone around her. Defiant dependence describes the behavior when someone resents having to be dependent on another, and out of that resentment acts out against them (see Chapter 20). Jenna was extremely defiantly dependent upon Linda and Bill. With three other children besides Jenna, Linda was exhausted, and she believed that her husband Bill enabled Jenna, allowing her to wallow in her excuses by not holding her accountable for her actions.

Bill just couldn't stand to see Jenna suffer the consequences of her behaviors in school or with her friends. He listened to Jenna's excuses, and he believed them. He felt so sorry for her when she would mope and wallow in self-pity after she had destroyed friendships due to her behavior, behavior that Jenna was either unwilling or unable to change in spite of years of counseling. Bill felt very strongly that Linda was pushing their daughter way too hard. Linda admittedly knew she was pushing Jenna very hard.

Linda was seeing her own counselor and had concluded that she had to 'let go' of what she could not control. She knew that she could no longer be part of enabling her daughter to continue her destructive behavior caused by the personality disorder. When Bill bailed Jenna out of jail for the third time, Linda was furious. She put her foot down, telling Bill that he HAD to see her counselor so he would understand how he was enabling Jenna to be sick. Bill was unwilling to do so. Repeatedly the two of them argued about what is too much and what is too little. And in the meantime, their daughter Jenna continued her self-destructive behavior.

*A bit of reflection:*

Was Linda pushing too hard? Or was Bill allowing Jenna to wallow in excuses, thus enabling her?

_____

_____

_____

_____

## Learn How to Contribute in Appropriate and Healthy Ways

Have you found yourself pushing too much or too little? What can you change? Put in writing one or two action plans that you will work on to improve.

_____

_____

_____

_____

How do you know when you are pushing your loved one too hard vs. allowing your loved one to wallow in their excuses?

_____

_____

_____

_____

How can you tell when your loved one honestly cannot do something vs. when they are merely using their mental health diagnosis as an excuse for not moving forward? What's too much and what's too little?

_____

_____

_____

_____

## Holding to Hope

There are no easy answers when it is too much and when is it too little.

**Thus, our third Fresh Hope Principle for those who are loved ones is:**

*At times I don't understand my loved one and can allow them to either wallow in their excuses, or push them too hard. Therefore I choose to learn healthy, appropriate ways to contribute to my loved one's recovery.*

### The Teeter-Totter of Too Much or Too Little

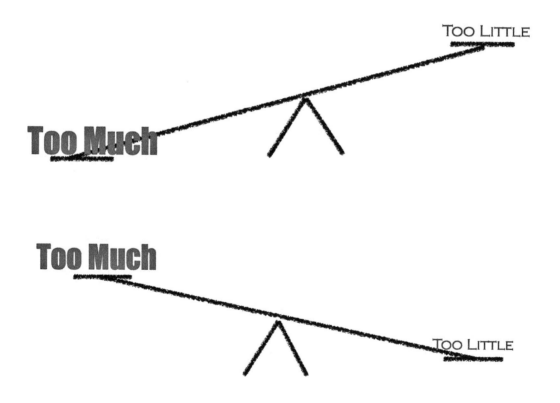

But there are some basic principles to find the balance that is "just right".

There are no standard answers for what is too much vs. too little. It is very difficult to know when you need to push/encourage your loved one to move forward in their recovery, versus when your loved one is not able to do something.

For example, Mary, a young woman with severe depression and mother of two small children, is struggling to get out of bed in the morning. Her husband is frustrated and angry about it, so he is constantly on her about how she should just pull up her bootstraps and force herself. Mary may not even be able to force herself to function until the depression she is experiencing begins to be treated. A mental illness can become debilitating, paralyzing just as a stroke can be. But also, the person who is suffering has to push forward, choose to do that which seems impossible to do. This is quite trying for Mary's husband to understand. He can demand too much and possibly make the depression worse, or not expect anything from her – only to allow her to become totally absorbed by the depression. Mary's husband is in that difficult time of learning what too much is vs. what is 'just right' in his expectations of his wife. He could push too much, leading Mary to feel so desperate as to end her life. While it is terribly difficult to figure out what how much and too little might be, it is terribly important in helping your loved one. And as they recover, this will change.

(Donna) Following Brad's manic episode in 1995, he became very agoraphobic. Getting him to leave the house was next to impossible. Even when he would try just to go outside to the backyard, he would suffer a debilitating panic attack. This was challenging for me to know when to push him to get out or if I should allow him to just be. A friend came from out of state to try and get Brad to go on a walk. Brad went, but only lasted five or six blocks before having to head back home. It was extremely difficult, as Brad's imprisonment was difficult on our entire family. I was carrying all of the responsibilities of caring for the kids and running the home. My husband was not functioning at all. He was not going outside of the house, and he was not eating.

At this point, I decided to push, but push using something I knew Brad used to love doing: going to Dairy Queen and having a hot fudge sundae. So I gave him advance notice one afternoon that at 2:30 pm we were going to the Dairy Queen and he had to go along. He had no choice. He had to go. I told Brad that the only decision he could make was which Dairy Queen he wanted to go to. So at 2:30 pm that afternoon I firmly told Brad to get up and come. He begged me not to make him. I was firm, but kind, and told him he *was* going. It took a bit, but finally we were on our way – to the farthest away Dairy Queen that Brad could think of. The entire way there he begged me to use the drive through and not make him go inside. I did agree, but made it clear that Brad understood that we would be doing this again, and the next time he had to go inside. We sat outside that Dairy Queen in our minivan and Brad ate a peanut buster parfait. It worked not only once, but numerous times where I pushed Brad to go with me to the Dairy Queen. Each time it got a bit easier. And it was the push that Brad needed.

*Learn How to Contribute in Appropriate and Healthy Ways*

---

Sometimes you need to push your loved one. And sometimes you need to not push but instead understand that they may not be able to do more than what they are doing. Small things that you encourage them to do may seem like very little steps, but they can make a huge difference. Donna pushing Brad to go to Dairy Queen was a seemingly simple thing. And after numerous visits to DQ, a number of peanut buster parfaits, and a few pounds later, Brad started to recover from the panic attacks.

*A bit of reflection:*

What are some things you might be able to with your loved one as Donna did with Brad?

_____

_____

_____

_____

What does 'contributing to my loved one's recovery' look like?

_____

_____

_____

_____

How do you learn to do that?

_____

_____

_____

_____

## In Your Own Words

*At times I don't understand my loved one and can allow them to either wallow in their excuses, or push them too hard. Therefore I choose to learn healthy, appropriate ways to contribute to my loved one's recovery.*

Rewrite Principle #3 in your own words, personalizing it for your situation:

_____

_____

_____

_____

## Devotional Reflection

The third part of Recovery Principle #3 is:

> Together we do better than trying on our own. We will hold one another accountable for learning, growing, and choosing to push through in hope.

> *"Therefore, encourage one another and build each other up."*
> *1 Thessalonians 5:11 (NIV)*

Knowing when to challenge someone with the expectations you have for them in their mental health recovery can be extremely difficult. Too few expectations may allow them to wallow in their excuses; too many could push them over the 'ledge'. No doubt, this is a significant cross to bear. Yet it is a key factor in you helping your loved one in their mental health recovery. (By the way, their doctor may be a great source of guidance when it comes to how much is too much or too little.)

Therefore, it's vitally important for you to ask your loved one for their forgiveness when you push too hard and expect too much or expect them to progress too fast. Even with your desire to not do harm to your loved one, sometimes even with the best of intentions and out of an abundance of love, we can still, and do, miss the mark. And instead of encouraging them and building them up, we are leaving them discouraged and weaker.

This Scripture, I Thessalonians 5:11, is so important for us in our relationship with our loved one. Learning to encourage them, to celebrate their accomplishments – even in seemingly small successes – is so major in building them up. So, how do you do it?

First, allowing the Lord to build you up through His Word, and secondly, through the support of others who understand and are safe, is key for your own healing and finding hope for this unchosen journey you find yourself on. It's when we feel His love and His encouragement that we being to look at our circumstances differently and find the courage, the hope, and the confidence to encourage our loved one. And when we have that ourselves, we can build our loved one up with hope, courage, and confidence for their journey of recovery.

There's great comfort to be found in Jesus' journey to the cross. Even as He prayed in the garden, He pleaded with His Father as He said, "My Father, if it is possible, may this cup be taken from Me. Yet not as I will, but as you will." His journey was not of His choosing. But He submitted Himself to His Father's will. And He 'built up' even those who crucified Him, when He asked the Father to forgive those who were putting Him to death.

## Look to Jesus

As you struggle upon through this unwanted journey you find yourself on, look to Jesus. Through Him, you will find the grace and mercy you need to have for your loved one and for yourself. At the cross you will find the patience, the love, and the desire to build up and encourage your loved one because you yourself will be filled with grace and forgiveness at the foot of the cross of Jesus.

### *Prayer:*

*Father, as you know, I've found myself on a journey that I never expected to be taking. I desperately need Your presence, Your peace, and Your grace to fill me. Please give me all that I need in the days ahead. Give me the wisdom to know when to lay out clear expectations of my loved one. Give me the wisdom to know when I must wait patiently with expectations as my loved one suffers. Give me the wisdom and insight to know the balance of these two.*

*The truth is Lord, this is scary, overwhelming, and so hard! Sometimes I want to pull out my hair! I desperately need You to fill my mind and my heart with the peace that passes all understanding. Give me the gift of encouragement for my loved one. Help me to find creative and meaningful ways to build up my loved one.*

*Lord, I can't do this alone. But with You I can do all things. So by the power of your Holy Spirit, lead me to contribute to my loved one's recovery in ways that only you can do. Help me to be my loved one's greatest cheerleader in their journey of hope and healing.*

*In Jesus' name. Amen.*

## Chapter 7

# Set Boundaries and Choose Hope

*Hope is a Choice In Spite of the Circumstances*

Austin was always a gifted, caring kid. But when his teenage years set in, it was as though someone had kidnapped Austin and replaced him with a moody, overly-sensitive, angry teen who for very brief and infrequent times, could be caring and fun.

Initially his parents, Don and Chris, figured it was just Austin being a teenager. However, by his sophomore year, it was obvious to Don and Chris that something more was going on with Austin. He was having a lot of trouble in school. And even more troubling to his parents were the friends he started hanging around with. They were drinking and using a lot of pot. Outbursts of anger and rage filled the next years of Austin's teens. Yet, he could turn around and he could be his previous loving self. It was a rollercoaster for his parents. One night, Don and Chris got a call that Austin had been detained by police, and were asked to come to a local mental health hospital.

When the police picked him up, Austin had been marching up and down the street, yelling and screaming and raging frantically in some sort of psychotic break. Austin ended up that night in the hospital, his first of many to come. Austin was diagnosed with bipolar disorder. He seemed accepting of it and he began taking the medicine. His mom and dad were happy again and thrilled to have life returning to normal. They thought they had their son back.

But as Austin grew older in his teens, he developed a cycle of taking his meds and doing well, and then going off his meds or using pot while he was on his meds. Several times, Austin ended up back in the hospital. He also ended up in jail several times. He ran away a number of times.

It seemed that a consistent part of Austin's storyline and journey was that he would refuse to stop using pot. He felt the pot was making him better, so of course he refused to stop using. And the more he used, the more he began to exhibit psychosis on a regular basis, which is not uncommon for young people who use pot before the age of 25. Austin got a new diagnosis when he was 20, schizoaffective disorder. By this point, there were so many hospital stays, times when he had run away, and times in jail that his parents could no longer handle it, or having him live at home.

Mom was having panic attacks about it all. Dad had lost his job and was now on anti-depressants. Austin's parents had been on a rollercoaster ride with him far too long, and it was time to stop the ride. If they were going to be able to endure long term and be there for their son, they couldn't ride that rollercoaster with him. Mom and Dad believed, with all their hearts, if they got their son to the right doctor, on the right medicine, and if he would stop using pot, that would be the answer. And he could have his life back instead of just this cycle of a rollercoaster.

They came to the realization that they couldn't fix their son, due to his continual choices of self-destructive behavior. They came to the realization that this is going to be a long-term issue. And in order to survive it and be of any help to their son, they needed to get off the rollercoaster and work on those issues. So they helped Austin find a new place to live. As, expected, things continued to get worse for

Austin. But for the first time, Mom and Dad were able to be there for him at their best, and they could get some breathing room from the issues at hand.

*A bit of reflection:*

How do you think that Austin's non-compliance may have caused conflicts within Don and Chris' relationship?

_____

_____

_____

_____


Wanting your loved one to do what they need to do to get and stay better can be extremely frustrating. Have you ever felt this way with your loved one? What do you do with those frustrations?

_____

_____

_____

## Set Boundaries and Choose Hope

When Don and Chris came to the realization that they couldn't fix their son, why was it important that they set boundaries for themselves to preserve their own sanity?

_____

_____

_____

_____

Within your own situation, how are your boundaries with your loved one? What might you need to work on?

_____

_____

_____

_____

When the one you love is doing well, you're doing better. When they are not doing well, you're super vigilant and not doing very well either. Riding the ups and downs of our loved one's recovery can take the life right out of us. It is incredibly exhausting to ride on their rollercoaster of recovery. It's all too easy to be happy when they are doing well, yet holding your breath that it lasts this time and wondering if and when there will be another episode. It's so easy to become hypervigilant about medicine, doctor appointments, therapist appointments, too much sleep, too little sleep, or fear of the phone call. After all, you are the caregiver, and your loved one has the illness. But the truth is, their illness can make you sick, too.

**Thus, our fourth Fresh Hope Principle for Loved Ones is:**

*At times I also feel hopeless, letting my loved one's actions and recovery define my happiness. Therefore, I choose to live with healthy emotional boundaries, and I choose my own joy despite the ups and downs of my loved one.*

Austin's parents came to the realization that they needed to set up emotional and physical boundaries with Austin. Otherwise, they would become distraught and emotionally wiped out themselves if they stayed on his cyclical rollercoaster ride. It would have been one thing if Austin was being compliant with the treatment and doing what was necessary for his schizoaffective disorder. If he was being compliant and still not doing well, it would have been important to keep him in their home, at least until he would become stabilized. But due to his own treatment self-sabotage, they had to separate themselves from him and the consequences of his choices. It was the healthy thing to do. They needed boundaries and a life that was not so enmeshed with Austin so they could actually be emotionally healthy in being there for their son.

Through the years we have met countless parents whose teen or young adult child were not taking their meds and acting out, and the parents were beyond frustrated, angry, and scared for their child. Their children were being defiantly dependent. Because the parents were so scared and worried about setting too hard of a boundary with their child, their child – who was mentally ill – was determining the boundaries. These parents had lost their leverage in helping their young adult make the right decisions. Instead, they were constantly softening the blows of their kid's behavior.

*Set Boundaries and Choose Hope*

---

When you don't set clear emotional boundaries with your loved one, you emotionally entangle yourself with them, and may end up becoming sick yourself. We've seen many loved ones come to Fresh Hope who are frazzled, worn out, spiritually and physically drained, and feeling hopeless. Many have ended up needing to take medication to help them cope with the exhaustion of loving someone with a mental illness.

Being emotionally enmeshed with someone is not compassion, nor is it empathy. You feel what they feel and experience, and you can lose yourself in the process. It's unhealthy for both of you. Emotional enmeshment with the one you love can enable them to stay sick and get even sicker, plus you can easily become sick because of it. That's because hopelessness is catching. When your loved one is not doing well and becomes hopeless (the loss of a future), then you as a caregiver will become hopeless, too, without appropriate healthy boundaries in place (see Chapter 4). It takes sheer emotional grit for you just to love this one who is struggling with a mental illness. Your brain chemistry will also be challenged if you don't separate yourself emotionally from the utter chaos and the emotional turmoil of the mental illness itself.

Setting boundaries can be very difficult to do. If you have a defiant young adult living with you, then a difficult but necessary boundary may need to be that if they aren't taking their medicine and doing what they need to get better, then they can no longer live in your home. Yes, that's a hard boundary to set, because your young adult child may become homeless. But it also may be the one boundary that allows them to feel the sting of their choices, and if the sting is great enough, they may finally decide they need to do what is necessary for getting better. Unfortunately, we usually don't decide to do the work of getting better until the pain of staying sick is greater than the pain of getting better.

(Donna) After Brad's manic episode became public news, many folks wondered why I chose to stay with him. Some of my friends encouraged me to leave Brad. But I knew I wasn't going to leave. What they didn't know is that I had set a very clear boundary early in the crisis. I told him that I knew who he was separate of the bipolar disorder. I assured him, 'I'm here to do what I can. As long as you do what you need to do to get better and stay well, I'm not leaving.' Brad admits being given this very clear and tough boundary was motivation for him to succeed.

And so, when Brad relapsed seven years later, it was extremely difficult on our marriage. Brad had been doing everything possible to live well. He especially had been very faithful at taking his medicines. But he had not necessarily learned enough about bipolar to realize that his mood could actually push pass the mood stabilizer. He also didn't know that stress could set off a significant mood swing. Put simply, he didn't know what he didn't know.

We were facing a lot of stress due to a variety of situations, including our nephew's debilitating bus accident and our church moving to a new location, which was triggering issues from prior to his first episode. Brad became depressed, nasty, and argumentative. This is dysphoric mania, which is mixed emotions. We want you to know that **it's not only negative situations that trigger a mood change**. Positive events like a move to a new house can also cause stress.

Brad mistakenly took his mood stabilizer twice one evening and realized when he was dizzy and foggy the next day. His greatest mistake was not immediately informing his doctor. Instead, Brad figured that if had taken a double dose, then to go without it the next night only made sense. Little did he know that mood stabilizers are out of the body in 24 hours. Brad knows that his moods escalate in the spring, but thought the medications would contain the mania. But stress can still cause mania. By the next night the mania was making decisions for him. Brad admits he doesn't remember much of those two weeks, but they resulted with another situation that yet again hit the local news media. Brad ended up in the hospital – and I was furious! I was so angry that Brad hadn't told me what was going on so we could have contacted the doctor and avoided another painful manic episode.

This was such a challenge for me and the boundary I had set seven years earlier. It was not easy at all. It took a lot of strength, courage, faith and a whole lot of forgiveness. And with that I restated the boundary plus a caveat: that I could not do this again. Another situation of pain and hurt as this would be too much.

This was another hard boundary set for Brad. And I made it clear that if Brad was not doing all that he could to stay well, that was not going to be an option.

(Brad) OK. She was not going to be riding the bipolar rollercoaster with me. But her boundary is exactly what I needed to push myself to do all that I could to be and to stay well. It was not at all an easy thing for Donna to do. But setting the boundary was key.

After the relapse is when I began to seriously research bipolar disorder. I reached into some deep places through therapy that helped me discover why my mania played out as it did. I started attending support groups for those who had a mental illness. I was desperately looking for hope, but wasn't finding much, especially through the groups. This is when the seed was planted to start Fresh Hope®.

It was Donna's clear boundaries and firm love that provided the frame work for my recovery. For the first time since being diagnosed, the relapse provided us with the ability to see that together, both of us were fighting the same monster. And the monster's name was not Brad, but the monster's name was bipolar disorder.

It is imperative for you to develop healthy emotional boundaries for yourself. The good news is that it is never too late to do this.

*So, how does one create emotionally healthy boundaries and hold to hope in spite of the hopelessness of a difficult circumstance?*

First, you have to decide that you won't allow your loved one's actions and recovery to define your happiness. Setting clear, healthy emotional boundaries will empower you to choose your own joy despite the ups and downs of your loved one. The word 'despite' in that sentence is key. Your being able to have joy and emotional wholeness despite your loved one's ups and downs is the sign of healthy emotional boundaries. It does not mean you lack compassion or empathy. It does not mean that you won't feel sad or discouraged at times. What it does mean is that you will not allow circumstances to affect your hope and your faith and your endurance. In other words, how you feel doesn't determine whether or not you have hope. You choose hope in spite of *how* you might feel or in spite of *what* might be going on with your loved one. You might feel hopeless, but you choose hope in spite of it.

**Develop healthy emotional boundaries for yourself**

**What might be considered enabling behaviors?**
- When you are willing to work harder on their recovery than they are
- When you make excuses for them instead of holding them accountable
- When you avoid confronting and holding them accountable
- When you keep peace at all cost, which isn't peace at all

*[If you are going through this book as a group, pause here and add to the list.]*

**What might be signs of you doing more work on their recovery than they are?**

First and foremost, **you need to provide yourself with care**. That simply means you need to do things that 'put into' you. As a caregiver, you are constantly giving out. Without putting back into yourself, you become depleted. Taking time away from your loved one is necessary. Doing things that refresh you, like just taking a nap and taking an afternoon for relaxing is a necessity. Allowing yourself not to think about your loved one for a period of time is essential. You may need to be creative in order to this.

Secondly, it's important to **understand how hopelessness and hope work**, and how you can stand on your faith in regards to having hope for your loved one and yourself 'despite' where they may – or may not be – in their recovery.

Thirdly, **exercise your faith faithfully**.

(Brad) A number of years ago, I joined a health club. It was a very nice two-story facility. The top floor was where the exercise equipment and exercise classes were held. On the first floor were an indoor and outdoor pool, steam room, sauna, hot-tub, and a snack bar. I belonged there approximately two years and had not lost one pound. In fact, I had gained a few pounds!

Donna was always curious as to why the health club wasn't helping me in my weight struggle. I was going on a regular basis, I knew a lot of people there, and had made a lot of friends. I was very familiar with the hot-tub, the steam room, and the outdoor swimming pool. I had a good tan, and was well known at the snack bar. I even knew my account number by heart to charge my food, but never once in those two years had I been upstairs to the exercise equipment, much less attend an exercise class. I wasn't exercising. I was snacking, and using the hot-tub and lying by the outdoor pool!

Why do we share this story? Because this is how a lot of Christians are in regards to their faith. They join the club – in other words, they go to church – but they never go upstairs so to speak, to exercise their faith.

Fourth, **see your future as good**. This is key to having hope. A good future can't be defined by your loved one's recovery. You need to grasp that you are not fully responsible for your loved one's behavior. If your loved one is an adult, you can't treat them as a child.

Fifth, **choose joy**. Yep, you read that right. Joy! So often we allow our circumstances to dictate our quotient of joy and hope. We end up feeling our circumstances instead of choosing joy over our circumstances. In spite of the most difficult and dire circumstances, we can have joy. Joy, because no matter how difficult life becomes or is, we know that all is well because of the Lord. Joy in spite of the fact that all might not be good, but all is well no matter what. And yes, it really is a choice. It's a matter of infusing our emotions and feelings with our faith – and not our circumstances. Choosing joy is key. Choosing to surround yourself with joy-filled people is also key. After all, joy, like hope, is catching!

> **Choose joy**

Understanding that the ups and downs of your circumstances need not become the dictator of how much joy and hope you have in your 'tank' is a determining factor in your understanding that you have a future. Your circumstances need not define your happiness. How well your loved one is doing or not doing need not dictate the amount of joy or hope you feel. Set this boundary in stone! Choosing to have hope, knowing there is a future, is what this tenet is all about. Having a future for YOU is a key to your hope.

## In Your Own Words

Rewrite Principle #4 in your own words, personalizing it for your situation:

_____

_____

_____

_____

## Devotional Reflection

The third part of Recovery Principle #4 is:

> Together we remind each other that our hope and joy come from the Lord. He alone is able to fulfill our needs in every aspect of our lives.

*"For I know the plans I have for you, declares the LORD, plans to prosper you and not to harm you, plans to give you hope and a future."*
*Jeremiah 29:11 (NIV)*

There is great comfort in knowing that our hope and joy come from the Lord and not from our circumstances. In fact, our joy and hope come from the Lord *in spite of* our circumstances. Hope especially is found in the fact that the Lord can take our circumstances, as difficult as they may be, and use them for our good! In spite of how difficult the many challenges of life can be, God is good and He is with you and He won't leave you. He has good plans for you, in spite of what you are presently going through.

Now let's be honest. It's important for us to remember that our original sin is rooted in what Satan said to Adam and Eve, that if they would eat of the tree of the knowledge of good and evil they would be like God. At the core of our sinful brokenness is that we believe we know what should happen and how it should happen. So it's important for us, especially as caregivers, to let go of control and the belief that we know how things should be, especially with the one we love who is suffering. We can want recovery for them; but we can't make them recover. We must trust the Lord in His promises and the plans and hope He has for our loved one.

Remember, the Lord alone fulfills us. Our possessions, our situations in life, our joy and hope are not due to our circumstances. They all come from the Lord. So when things don't look good, we put our hope in the Lord. We choose to exercise our faith in Him, not in things that surround us. We choose to flex our faith muscles within the most difficult situations. And we don't stop. We keep exercising our faith step by step, moment by moment, not giving up, not shutting up, and not putting up! We simply stay steady in faith and drawing even closer to the Lord. Like Max Lucado's mantra we discussed in Chapter 3 – it isn't easy and will take longer than we want, but we *will* get through it. And as we go through it, we choose to find our joy and hope in the Lord and not in our circumstances.

**Prayer:**

*Jesus, I so desperately want my loved one to recover from what they are going through that I have wanted to control them, the situation, and even to tell You what to do. My joy and hope are strong when they are doing well and it all falls apart when they aren't doing well. Lord, honestly, it's really hard to find my hope and joy in You in the midst of this crisis that my loved one and I, and many others, are going through. It's so hard to look at the circumstances and not take control, or not become discouraged and frustrated. I need Your help. Please, please help me to look to You. Please, by the power of Your Holy Spirit, empower me to exercise my faith.*

*The truth is, Lord, I know that in the midst of the difficulties of this life is when you build up our spiritual muscles. Sometimes those muscles are aching from my flexing them so much. Keep me focused on You. Keep me focused on the hope that You have given. Keep me focused on Your plans which are full of hope and a wonderful future.*

*My hope is built on nothing less than You, Jesus. This is my sure and certain hope that You will take all things and work them out together for my good, in spite of what I see with my earthly eyes.*

*Jesus, please hear my cry. And in the meantime, strengthen me to continue to trust in You for my hope and joy.*

*In Your Holy Name. Amen.*

## Chapter 8

# Your Loved One Needs A Healthy and Encouraging You

*Become the Best You Possible*

Both in their early twenties, it was now just the two of them: Abby and Liz. Three years earlier they lost both parents in a car accident. Ever since, Liz has not been the same. Abby, on the other hand, has been able to grieve and move forward. Liz has just lost her job due to her depression; missing too many days of work. Abby has been more than frustrated with Liz, and has lost her cool a few too many times. Abby keeps telling her sister what she needs to do to get out of the depression, and can't understand why Liz doesn't listen to her. She'd like to give Liz a swift kick in the butt. At wit's end, Abby decided to disengage emotionally. Despite being roommates, she now ignores her sister's issue and offers no emotional support. It is Liz's problem to figure out.

Months go by, and the sisters seldom interact. Liz sank even deeper into the endless pit of depression and despair. Abby went about her living miffed that Liz was too stubborn to heed her only sister's answers. Abby continued to be disengaged; that is, until Liz's suicide attempt. While Liz was in the hospital, one of the counselors confronted Abby at the family meeting, telling her that she was going to have to learn how to help her sister. The counselor explained that Liz didn't need her to have all of the answers, and was able to help Abby understand that she needed to find different ways to provide support to encourage Liz. Fortunately, Abby was willing to re-engage in the relationship, having learned new ways to relate to and help Liz in her recovery. Slowly, Liz is improving. Abby is relating to her sister in new ways that are more helpful. It's not been an easy road for either of them, but they are learning, growing, and moving forward.

*A bit of reflection:*

What were the two approaches that Abby attempted to take with her sister? Why did neither of them work?

_____

_____

_____

_____

How do you think Liz felt when Abby was telling her what to do? How do you think Liz felt when Abby ignored her situation?

_____

_____

_____

_____

In what ways can you relate to Abby? Why? In what ways might you have contributed to the dysfunctional ways of your loved one's recovery?

_____

_____

_____

_____

Abby seemed to 'let go' and gave up on her sister. How do you 'let go' without giving up? (Changing what you can and knowing what you can't change.)

_____

_____

_____

_____

What is the difference between having all of the answers, and encouraging someone?

_____

_____

_____

_____

Does your loved one need you to be involved? In what ways and to what extent?

How easy it for you to become part of the dysfunctional living that mental health issues have caused for your loved one? Examples?

What new ways of relating and encouraging have you discovered that has helped your loved one? What have discovered doesn't work?

Do you see the need in your own life to learn new behaviors and relating to your loved one? Why?

_____

_____

_____

_____

Abby's frustration and deciding to disengage from her sister is a very real issue for those of us who are loved ones. It's easy to lose our patience and raise our voices out of desperation. We can easily get triggered by our loved one's actions and decisions that can cause dysfunctions within our relationship. Plus, any type of dysfunctional issues that were there prior to the onset of a mental health issue can become even more difficult as a result. As loved ones, we not only learn about mental illnesses and how to relate to our loved ones, but we also learn a lot about ourselves and find we need to learn new things about our own behaviors and thinking.

**Thus, our fifth Fresh Hope Principle for those who are loved ones is:**

*I, too, have been part of the cycle of dysfunctional living, either thinking I had all the answers or thinking the problem didn't belong to me. Therefore, I choose to submit myself to learning new behaviors and taking responsibility for my own healthy, balanced living.*

Research shows that when a person with a mental illness has the positive and encouraging involvement of those who love them, they get better faster and usually stay better longer. But the opposite would also be true. If someone with a mental illness does not have any support, or the support they have is hurtful or negative, they will most likely stay sick longer.

(Donna) I knew I needed to be there for our kids. I did my best, but didn't do as much as I felt I should. At first, I talked with Brad's secretary (whose first day on the job was the day of the first incident). But that put her in a difficult position, still being employed at the church. I had a counselor friend who betrayed confidentiality in a public meeting. Here was someone I thought to be a safe place to pour out my despair, and it was used against me. I had a lot of people I thought I could trust. But after many hurtful situations, I learned that I couldn't. I knew I had people I could call if we were in a financial bind, but emotionally, I had no one to talk with who would truly understand.

**Self-care is not selfish**

The healthier you are emotionally and spiritually, the better the contributor you become for your loved one's successful recovery. You don't have all of the answers – and you don't need to. Part of the beauty of what happens in support groups such as Fresh Hope is that you can get a lot of ideas and answers from others who are facing similar types of challenges as you and your loved one. One way to learn new ways of thinking and new behaviors is by processing them in a support group and or with a therapist.

It's so important to remember to care for yourself. Self-care is not selfish. Just like when you fly, they tell you to put on your oxygen mask first, and then you put the mask on those who need your help. Applying that practice to your situation, it's imperative for you to find your own emotionally and spiritually healthy balance to be the most helpful to your loved one. You might want to list ways to care for yourself and keep it handy, track what you are doing for self-care, and note what works best for you. Self-care may even include you needing to take medicine for the stress you are under. It's not all that common for the loved ones to become clinically depressed due to the situation. It's called situational depression. Donna has taken an anti-depressant occasionally throughout the years due to situational depression.

Through the years of being a part of our own Fresh Hope group we have seen time and time again where the stress of the loved one's mental health struggle has taken its toll on their husband or wife, mom or dad, etc. An ongoing difficult, stressful life situation can easily cause depression and/or anxiety. When any situational difficulties in life are intense and/or drawn out, many people will struggle with depression, anxiety, and even trauma. It is totally understandable, and there is help and hope for this, too. This may mean that you as the loved one may need to take medicine for a time. There's no shame in this! After all, we tell those we love who have a mental health diagnosis that there is no shame in them taking their medicines or seeing a doctor; so why do we exclude ourselves from the very thing we believe is best for our loved ones? If taking medicine and seeing a doctor is good for those we love, then it must be true for those of us who are the loved ones.

When someone you love has a mental illness life can become extremely unpredictable and unbalanced. You can end up spending every single ounce of your focus, time, and energy on caring for them that there is little time left for yourself or others in your family. Therefore, it's so important for you to practice selfcare. Remember Tenet 4? It is about leading a healthy, balanced life. Here are some simple ways to practice self-care (some to do alone and some to do with someone who is life-giving to you):

- Exercise or walk daily

- Go out for coffee or lunch with a friend
- Do whatever you really enjoy doing (Example: for Donna, she likes to kayak)
- Spend quiet time with the Lord, meditating on His Word
- Attend a support group
- Read a book (not on mental illness) for fun
- Watch a series on Netflix
- Take a nap

Many more things could be added to this list. It's important for you to have a plan of what works for you, replenishes you, and refreshes you.

What are practical ways to submit yourself to learning new behaviors and new ways to relate to your loved one? Here's a few that we can think of:

- Read a book about mental health issues, especially reading about others' journeys can give great insight to new ways to love the one who in your life has a diagnosis.
- Attend a mental health support like Fresh Hope. Within a healthy mental health support group, you can gain great insight into mental illness and new ways to relate to your loved one. And if no Fresh Hope group meets in your community, you can attend one online. (www.FreshHopeMeeting.com)
- Identify someone who has lived what you are going through, and spend time talking and processing with them on a regular basis.
- See a therapist.

Those are just a few ways to learn new behaviors and ways to relate to your loved one. What might you add to the list for yourself?

*Holding to Hope*

In order to not ride the recovery roller coaster of ups and downs in your own mental health due to the ups and downs of your loved one's struggle, it's imperative to care for yourself, to set boundaries, and not to determine your joy and happiness based upon how your loved one is doing. This involves your own self-care and learning about their illness/disorder to find the best ways of interacting with them that will help them in their recovery.

## In Your Own Words

Rewrite Principle #5 in your own words, personalizing it for your situation:

_____

_____

_____

_____

## Devotional Reflection

The third part of Recovery Principle #5 is:

> Together we choose freedom over suffering, and joy in living through self-knowledge in action.

*"We demolish arguments and every pretension that sets itself up against the knowledge of God and we take captive every thought to make it obedient to Christ." 2 Corinthians 10:5*

## *A bit of reflection:*

2 Corinthians 10:5 is a passage that hits us squarely between the eyes of our pride. We sinful human beings have at our core brokenness the 'desire to be like God'. In other words, we like to think we have the answers and how things should be. Remember what Satan said to Adam and Eve in the Garden? He said, "Eat this, and you will be like God!" They were eating from the tree of the knowledge of good and evil. And since then all us, including you, struggle with believing that we have the answers and know how things should be. Yet Paul, reminds us here that we don't have the answers, and that we need to support our thinking to the very words and promises of the Lord.

In order to choose emotional freedom from the ups and downs of the suffering that we and the one we love who has a mental health diagnosis, we must think and see it as the Lord sees it. That's where true freedom from the mental illness roller coast lies. Freedom does not lie in us. But when we take captive our thinking, aligning it with the Word of God, we suddenly, by the power of the Holy Spirit, can do all things in Christ who gives us strength – even the strength for a journey such as this one we find ourselves on.

## *Prayer:*

*Lord, I have at times been part of the problem. Often, I have thought I had all the answers for my loved one's recovery, believing that I knew how it should be. And in frustration at times, I washed my hands of it and thought that their recovery had nothing to do with me, so I wanted to just walk away from it. And neither is true. You and you alone have the answers. So I look to you, Lord.*

*Show me, teach me new attitudes, new ways of seeing things and even new ways that I might contribute in a healthy and helpful way to my loved one's recovery.*

*Show me, teach me new ways of caring for myself that refresh me according to the ways that You have created me. And most of all Lord, show me, teach me, and empower me to align my thinking with Your word that I might even see the joy and purpose in a journey that involves struggle and pain.*

*In Jesus' Name. Amen.*

## Chapter 9

# Healed Heart Wounds Will Allow You to Move Forward

*Don't Let the Wounds Fester*

Scott had been successful as a businessman. He is a committed Christian, husband, and father, and he also has bipolar disorder. While he has achieved a lot of financial success in the jobs he has held, he has also had lots of job losses. Scott had been fired several times. He has also committed several sexual indiscretions. All this has been very tough for his wife and children to go through. But his wife, Julie, has hung-in-there with him. Scott's doctor was vital in helping Julie separate the difference between the man she loved and the bipolar disorder. So she was committed to making it work as long as Scott was willing to do his part. Naturally, Julie had some hurt, anger, fear, and bitterness, but she was also a strong woman of faith and believed that the Lord could get them through all of the pain.

About seven years ago, Scott experienced the turning point in his recovery journey. He had a manic episode, which resulted in him being fired, and he ended up with a lengthy hospital stay. Following the hospitalization Scott still faced a very long period of depression. It took him a long time to start to 'get up and live', but he began to discover ways to live well and a faith-filled life in spite of having bipolar disorder. He found that he could manage the bipolar disorder instead of it controlling him. Since that episode, Scott has been living symptom-free. He is once again the man that Julie had fallen in love with, but Julie is still filled with anger and resentment.

Julie is madder than hell, and rightfully so. While saying she would stick it out, she did only that. It was as though she bunkered down and by sheer grit and faith plowed through. Everyone marveled at her strength. But as she went through it, her focus was so much on Scott and keeping the family together that her feelings and hurt were pushed to the side. Now she finds herself angry and resentful towards Scott. She feels guilty about her feelings, because she thought she had forgiven him. But as Scott was working on his recovery, Julie wasn't working through her anger and resentment. In actuality, she had decided with her head to forgive, but her heart had also been wounded. And those wounds had yet to be treated.

Julie knew in her head that her husband's behaviors were a direct result of him having bipolar disorder. But she still didn't like feeling like a victim of so many hurtful things that Scott had said and done. Scott was doing well, but she wasn't. She realized it was time to process her heart wounds so that she, too, could live well. She made an appointment to see a counselor. Julie was ready to have heart wounds healed.

***A bit of reflection:***

How do you think Julie was feeling?

_____

_____

_____

_____

*Healed Heart Wounds Will Allow You to Move Forward*

While Julie was trying to do the Christian 'right thing', it was hurting her. Why?

_____

_____

_____

_____

Have you found yourself in a situation like Julie's, or feeling like Julie? How angry are you at issues in your relationship because of the mental health issue?

_____

_____

_____

_____

What are some unhealed heart wounds that you have due to the mental health challenges of your loved one?

_____

_____

_____

_____

Unhealed heart wounds that have been caused by the mental health challenges of your loved one can and most likely will hold you back. So often we easily believe that we have either worked through the hurt, yet in truth we have only been stuffing it. Many times we intellectually apply spiritual truths to the wound, as in the case of Julie. She stuffed the hurt from the wound and chose forgiveness, only to find that wound was festering resentment within her. She chose the Christian thing to do, but didn't deal with the wound, and the wound was getting worse. Of course, there are times where you have to go about doing the Christian and the 'right' things, setting aside your needs and heart wounds for the moment to deal with the crisis of your loved one. But at some point, you need to tend to your wound.

In many ways, this goes back to what we talked about in Chapter 3. When you don't deal with your pain, your pain deals with you. Think of it this way: let's say you have a physical wound such as a deep cut on your arm. But you do nothing about it. You don't even work to stop the bleeding. What might happen? Do you run the risk of bleeding out? Infection? Losing the arm? Or even potentially dying? Or let's say that you broke your leg, but did nothing about it. One can only imagine what issues might come about when trying to walk. Heart wounds are no different than physical wounds. You must attend to them at some point. Maybe you can't do this immediately as you address your loved one's needs, but sooner rather than later, you must tend to your heart wounds. If not, just as Julie realized, they will all too soon cause issues.

> **When you don't deal with your pain, your pain deals with you**

**Thus, our sixth Fresh Hope Principle for those who are loved ones is:**

*At times, I have viewed myself as a victim of my loved one's behavior and disorder, living in resentment, anger, unforgiveness, or self-pity. Therefore,*

***I choose to separate the disorder from the person I love, forgive and let go of the past, and live as a contributor to successful recovery.***

Do you have some heart wounds due to your loved one's behavior or words? Or due to advocating for them? If so, have you processed those wounds? If not, why not? Has this been an issue for you to be able to move forward? Has this possibly been an issue for you to be a positive contributor to your loved one's successful recovery?

Heart wounds will cause you to feel like a victim of your loved one's behavior and disorder. And those heart wounds cause emotional and spiritual infections of resentment, anger, unforgiveness, and self-pity. Despite trying your best to intellectually choose the right response, the heart wound will sooner or later make you sick. Unfortunately, simply knowing with our head what the right choice is does not cause the heart wound to go away. Let's imagine someone behind you on a down escalator trips and falls on you, causing a chain reaction. You end up with a broken wrist and two fractured vertebrae. Being an accident, of course you forgive them, but you still must tend to the fractured wrist and vertebrae. You can't forgive them and pretend that nothing happened. The same is true of heart wounds.

You can make decisions with your head, but your heart holds the feelings and hurts. The head can't simply overrule the feelings. You can choose to not let something hurt you, but if your heart feels the sting of the hurt, then you have to deal with it. After all, you are only a human. Don't expect things of yourself that are truly things of God.

Let's be honest, the behaviors of those we love who have a mental illness can be very hurtful and painful, causing many heart wounds. We can know in our heads that their behavior is due to their mental illness. But knowing this does not take away the sting of their hurtful words and behaviors. If you don't address those wounds, those wounds will stand in the way of you being able to heal and move forward.

Stuffing or constantly setting aside your heart wounds because you think that your loved one is too sick or in too much of a crisis can only cause you to becoming overstuffed with unprocessed pain and hurt. If your loved one is too sick to be able to be part of your processing of heart wounds, then it is important that you tend to those heart wounds with someone, such as a counselor or your pastor. But there are certain times when it may be necessary for you to process the wounds with your loved one, as it may be a large part of their healing journey.

(Donna) After seven years of coping and working his recovery I was so angry that Brad had relapsed. With his first manic episode, I felt anger, but at the church leadership for not helping sooner. This time I was so, so angry at Brad (his bipolar disorder, really) for putting us through this again. He was in the hospital, and wanted me to take him clean underwear. But I wasn't ready to see him yet. I waited a day before I went! It took me a long time to get past that anger.

Let's be honest: there can be traumatic experiences you experience due to your loved one's mental illness. And it's so important for you to deal with the pain caused by those traumatic events, as much as you are able, without it causing even more trauma within your family. Sometimes it is important to share with your loved one the hurt and pain that you are feeling. But sometimes your loved one is too emotionally vulnerable at the time and so you need to find another way to express that hurt and pain. Taking all of your pain to the cross is always a must! Plus, learning how to lament to the Lord is very therapeutic.

As we discussed in Chapter 3, Scripture is full of Laments. Many of the Psalms are laments. The Lord created us with feelings and emotions, and He even encourages us to express them! Very simply, a lament is a complaint and cry out to God about a situation in which you first recognize who the Lord is and your faith in Him. Then you state the issue and cry out to Him to intervene, to change it, to take away your pain. You acknowledge to Him that He's the only one who can do this, and then you wait on Him. And you also tell the Lord that as you wait, you will trust Him for His perfect timing and will praise Him while you wait. The beauty of a lament is twofold: in lamenting you are able to express your feelings. Secondly, ending our laments with what we will do while we wait pivots our focus from the problem to focusing on the Lord, which in turn keeps us from merely ruminating about the problem.

Lamenting is good for you to do. We encourage you to speak it out loud to Him. Cry, shout, or moan, He understands. Pour out your emotions. This is all part of healing. It is the processing of your pain. And it is ever so necessary for your own healing. This empowers you to love your loved one without the resentment, anger, unforgiveness, and self-pity.

Understand that is it ever so important to separate the mental health disorder or illness from your loved one, just as you would do with any other physical illness. If your loved one had cancer, you wouldn't blame them for having it, nor would you blame your loved one for their inability to function as they had in the past. Unfortunately, with mental health illness the very organ that is sick is also making some of the decisions. It affects a person's behaviors. And those behaviors can become very troublesome. This is why it is called Behavioral Health. You might want to ask yourself, "If my loved one was in their 'right-mind', would they be acting this way? It helps to separate your loved from the mental illness and see them as their true selves, recalling them within their 'right-mind'. For example, when Brad relapsed, and Donna was so mad at him for "putting us through this again", it was really bipolar putting us through it again. Bipolar was in charge, not Brad. Brad was not in his 'right-mind'.

Please also understand that there are times when your loved one is too sick to make the right choices and/or behave in ways they would in their right-mind. Yes, there are times when choices early-on in the process of getting sick or prior to relapsing that your loved one can make choices that either will stop the illness from getting a stronger grip or at least lessen it, but sometimes that window is ever-so-short and small. It's complicated and calls for such balance on your part as we discussed in Chapter 6. But know this, as complicated and as difficult as it is to love someone with a mental illness, it becomes even more complicated and difficult if you are not dealing with your own emotions and pain. In other words, you then become negative force, a negative contributor to your loved one's healing. Therefore, it is imperative for you to be self-processing your wounds along the way to the best of your ability. Will you do it perfectly? No. No one can do it perfectly. When you fall short of it, ask for forgiveness, learn from it, and move on. Give grace to yourself also!

When you are living as your best self through your loved one's journey with a mental health challenge, you become a positive contributor to your loved one's recovery. But how? How can you contribute positively?

### *How to become a positive contributor of your loved one's recovery*

- Be the best 'you' possible – emotionally and spiritually.

- Tend to your heart wounds. Seek healing for them, either through seeing a therapist or your pastor, or consider attending a Trauma Healing class through Fresh Hope (More information at FreshHope.us). When you heal up your heart wounds, you will no longer feel like a victim; and resentment, anger, and self-pity won't be able to take deep root. Yes, it may take time, and it will be a process, but you will be able to move forward.

- Don't be afraid to grieve the fact that mental illness has struck your family and life has changed due to it.

- Separate your loved one from their disorder. This is an ongoing process, but love the person and fight together against the mental illness.

- Ask thoughtful and leading questions, instead of telling your loved one what to do.

- Cheer them on.

- Learn to communicate with your loved one about your heart wounds, at the appropriate time and way, speaking the truth in love. Too often we think we dare not add anything to their plate due to their struggle. But if shared at the right time and in the right way, it can contribute to their recovery.

## In Your Own Words

*At times, I have viewed myself as a victim of my loved one's behavior and disorder, living in resentment, anger, unforgiveness, or self-pity. Therefore, I choose to separate the disorder from the person I love, forgive and let go of the past, and live as a contributor to successful recovery.*

Rewrite Principle #6 in your own words, personalizing it for your situation:

_____

_____

_____

_____

## Devotional Reflection

The third part of Recovery Principle #6 is:

Together, we share in each other's victories and celebrate the whole person.

*For God has not given us a spirit of fear, but of power and love and a sound mind." 2 Timothy 1:7*

Learning how to celebrate the 'whole' person is so important. It's so easy for you and your loved one to become so focused on the mental health challenge you are both experiencing, that you forget about the wholeness of one another's personhoods as well as the 'wholeness' of your lives. There is more to your lives than what you are going through at the moment. There is more to your loved one than just their diseased brain. Remembering to celebrate the steps of healing within the journey is ever so important. But also remembering to celebrate the personhood of your loved one is incredibly important, too. Celebrate all those things you love about them. This builds them up in Christ. It also encourages them to have the courage to move forward not in fear, but in their sound mind!

**Celebrate the 'whole' person**

We have found through our years of marriage that forgiving one another is truly connected directly to our understanding and experiencing the love and forgiveness of the Lord. The more you understand how much the Lord loves you and how He has had mercy (not giving you what you do deserve) upon you, the easier it is for you to truly forgive your loved one.

*A bit of reflection:*

Are there any ways that you may have contributed or are contributing to your loved one's recovery in negative ways? If so, how have you or will you make amends for it with your loved one?

_____

_____

_____

_____

Are you processing your worries, hurts, and pains in appropriate ways as you take this journey along with your loved one? What things do you need to do in order to process/work through possible resentments, anger, and/or unforgiveness? (How about lamenting?)

_____

_____

_____

_____

How might you become even more of a contributor to your loved one's recovery?

_____

_____

_____

_____

**Prayer**:

*Lord, I come to you in the name of Jesus.*

*Forgive me Lord for the times I've contributed negatively to my loved one's recovery. Show me positive ways that I may contribute to their recovery. Fill me with your forgiveness, mercy, and love.*

*Lord, I also bring to you the wounds of my heart. I bring to you the cries of my heart. You understand my tears that I have cried. You understand the burdens I carry. By the power of Your Word and the Holy Spirit, continue to help me work through my own hurts and feelings regarding my loved one's journey. Only through You and Your Spirit will I have the courage, the power, and the love to face each and every day. Give to me a sound mind and a peace-filled heart.*

*Lord, give me insights for celebrating my loved one as a whole person. Give me the right words at the right time, words that encourage, build up, but also speak truth, even when it is hard to speak it.*

*Thank you for hearing me Lord.*
*In Jesus' name. Amen.*

## Chapter 10

# Giving Back Will Give Back to You

*Giving Back Creates Thriving in Spite of Your Circumstances*

Jane had been through hell and back with her mom. Jane started attending a Fresh Hope group out of desperation as to how to help her Mom survive her schizoaffective disorder. Her mom suffered a lot of psychosis, experienced long bouts of depression, and numerous suicide attempts. Jane found a lot of comfort, strength, encouragement, and hope in her Fresh Hope group.

They were now at the two-year mark. Her mom had not been hospitalized ever since the doctors had determined a working medicine combination. Jane was doing pretty well herself, so she decided that she didn't need the group anymore. She stopped attending for about three weeks. But she missed the group interaction and the boost it gave her. She didn't need anything more from the group, but she felt drawn to return.

While at the meeting, it dawned on Jane why she needed to go to the group. It was because she had something to offer to the new people in the group. Through sharing her journey, she loved being able to speak hope into other people's hopelessness. It made all the pain worth something more than just a learning experience. Jane realized she had a voice, and as she shared, that voice became liquid gold to those who desperately needed hope. While she didn't need the group to help her get through to the next week, she did need the group so that her pain would serve a true purpose in helping others. She also knew that the group needed her, and that kept her going. Not long after returning to the group she became a facilitator and ended up starting a group at her church. And to Jane's total amazement, her mom is her co-facilitator!

Out of Jane and her mom's painful journey has come a beautiful story of God's redemption of years of suffering, multiple hospitalizations, two jail stays and three suicide attempts. They have come to see and experience that they have a lot more to offer than they ever would have believed. And the incredible reward is that as Jane and her mom give back by leading a group, they keep getting stronger, more empowered, and their hope tank continues to overflow. It's amazing to them what the Lord is doing and has done with their pain and brokenness. They have come to know in a very real way that sharing and giving back is healing – for you and for others.

***A bit of reflection:***

Have you ever felt like you didn't have much to give, and surprisingly found out that what you did have to offer helped someone else?

_____

_____

_____

_____

*Giving Back Will Give Back to You*

Why do you think it might be important to give back after having been helped yourself?

_____

_____

_____

_____

Do you think you can give back too soon? When is the right time to start giving back?

_____

_____

_____

List some ways you might consider giving back.

_____

_____

_____

_____

When you share, it is healing for you and others. When you give to others, you become stronger. It helps you find your voice. Giving back empowers you. And it reaffirms your hope and insights, which in return builds resiliency. And you always, ALWAYS, have way more to offer than you think you do!

> **Giving back empowers you**

Just as Jane experienced along with her mom, their story filled with all of the pain and brokenness became liquid gold in helping others find hope in the midst of their pain and brokenness. They were offering the same comfort that had been offered to them.

(Donna) Each of us needs to discover the way we can give back, based on who we are. I've been through it and know how it feels. God has been very clear on what He wants me to be involved in. I'm a good 1-on-1 person in helping other loved ones. I also receive wonderful fulfillment leading Trauma Healing groups and training new Trauma Healing facilitators, being a Hope Coach and helping start the group, Surviving2gether, for loved ones of suicide.

According to EHN Canada, '*studies show that individuals in recovery that continue to help others find sobriety are more likely to stay abstinent than those who do not help others*' (edgewoodhealthnetwork.com, 2014). We believe that is also true with mental health recovery. We have seen it over and over since starting the first Fresh Hope group. After all, sharing – giving back – is also receiving. You end up receiving new and positive insights from helping others that makes you even stronger in your recovery.

According to Vantage Point (vantagepointrecovery.com, 2017):

> *"Giving back the right way has proven physical health benefits. It lowers blood pressure and reduces stress.*
>
> *You find yourself laughing more and having an enjoyable time at events you have a passion for. It is hard to have a negative outlook when you are laughing and having fun. Therefore, giving back the right way can reduce depression.*
>
> *Other physical traits associated with volunteering include being able to get better sleep and less anxiety.*
>
> *When you feel worthy and valuable, your mental health becomes stronger. Giving back or volunteering can give meaning to our lives, making us feel we have a purpose. Some research suggests it does so because giving back connects us to other people.*
>
> *When we build relationships and feel close to others, we get a sense of belonging. This leads us to feel important and that we are here for a reason. Usually that reason relates to helping others rather than a self-gratifying purpose."*

**Thus, our seventh Fresh Hope Principle for those who are loved ones is:**

***I, too, have become focused on my loved one's situation and how it has affected me. I can easily become so consumed by our issues that I fail to see those around me who would benefit from what I've learned. Therefore, I choose to give back by seeking opportunities to help others by sharing my insights and experiences.***

(Brad) Over the last 30 years, I've spent countless hours doing pastoral counseling with what seems to be a 'gazillion' or more individuals, couples, and families. I've heard just about everything and seen even more. I've witnessed what should be manageable problems tear families apart. Broken relationships, wounded people, discouragement, and despair seem all too familiar. But I have also watched families, couples, and individuals pull together and become stronger through overwhelming circumstances that I was sure no one could survive. They not only survived, but they thrived!

I've asked myself what it is that those who thrive in spite of horrible life-altering circumstances have, that those who seem done in by even less severe circumstance do not have? I have concluded that the 'thrivers' have certain qualities in common, and specifically one major thing. What is that one thing? They help others in spite of their circumstances. They regularly and consistently give and help other people in spite of their pain.

Helping and giving to others gives temporary relief to one's overwhelming circumstances. It has the power to cause a shift in one's perception of their problems. Time and time again I have seen people going through tragic events in their own lives step out of their pain to help someone else. By giving to others, their focus changes. When you and I help others in spite of what is going on in our lives, it has the power to change everything. When I move the focus off myself and onto someone else, if even for a brief moment, my personal pain is brought into focus.

It seems that when we lose our perspective due to our circumstances, the circumstances feel even worse. When we focus only on ourselves and how horrible our circumstances might be, we allow the circumstances to hold even more power and pain in our lives.

Giving and helping others in spite of what we might be going through is the release valve from the pressures of our circumstances. Just like a tea kettle, the pressure builds in our lives when the circumstances are difficult. There has to be a release of the build-up of the environmental pressure, or it leads to potential disaster.

As you are well aware, a mental health disorder/illness can be very challenging. It can cause difficult circumstances within one's life. It can cause your loved one to become very self-focused, (which at times is necessary). But, if the focus is only inward, then the mental health challenge has the potential to hold too much power in our lives.

*A bit of reflection:*

Do you find yourself focused only on you and your circumstances? If so, have you thought about helping someone else? List one or two ways you can help someone this week.

_____

_____

_____

_____

*Holding to Hope*

Have you found helping others to be good for you?

_____

_____

_____

_____

Put simply, giving back will give back to you. When you give back, you will find that what you receive from it will exceed what you put in. And because of it, your sharing will bring healing, help you find your voice, empower you, and raise your hope exponentially.

In fact, giving back on an ongoing basis may be just as important as deciding to get better. A sense of learned helplessness is often seen within the world of mental health care. Both those who have a mental illness and those who love them begin feeling helpless and dependent on others to help them as they struggle in their crisis. It's unknown territory for them, so help is needed. But if they only continue to be helped and look to others to tell them what to do and how to do it, they have learned helplessness. When someone takes ownership of their recovery, they become empowered – and even more so when they see they can help others going through the same things. It is really amazing to see it work.

### *Here are three extremely major lessons I (Brad) learned in starting Fresh Hope:*

1. When I facilitated the first Fresh Hope group, I was amazed at how fulfilling and strengthening it was. I became stronger and more resilient in my own recovery. After all, it is said that when you teach or lead, you often learn more than your students!

2. I didn't understand the power of real support groups. As a pastor, I had always approached changing lives from a perspective of teaching something, as opposed to with one another. That's why I am such an advocate for ongoing support groups, not class-type, specified-term groups. I have never seen lives changed so easily and so dramatically as when people share their stories (give back) to one another. (It's a sad truth that this core of the early Christian church has been lost. Over and over people tell us that their experience in a Fresh Hope group is how they feel the church should be.)

3. When someone decides to share their story in meaningful ways, publicly or semi-public, it empowers them like nothing has. When you share your pain and brokenness and your journey to healing, and it becomes insight for others, it is transformative. That's what Revelation 12:11 proclaims about the power of our testimony:

*They triumphed over him by the blood of the Lamb*
*and by the word of their testimony;*
*they did not love their lives so much as to shrink from death.* (NIV)

From our experience with Fresh Hope and seeing people begin to share their stories with one another, speaking hope into other people's situations, what happens is amazing. Those sharing their stories are simply sharing – but what their listeners receive is like a key to hope and a future. It is in these exchanges happening a multitude of times during a meeting that we see the power of giving back.

## In Your Own Words

Rewrite Principle #7 in your own words, personalizing it for your situation:

_____

_____

_____

_____

## Devotional Reflection

The third part of Recovery Principle #7 is:

> Together we recognize that sharing helps both us and others heal. Sharing helps us find our voice and becomes empowering as we see our pain redeemed by the Lord. As we share, it helps reaffirm our own hope while also giving hope away to others.

> ***"(The Lord) helps us in all our troubles, so that we are able to help others who have all kinds of troubles, using the same help that we ourselves have received from God." 2 Corinthians 1:4 (Good News Translation)***

Sometimes we spend way too much time focused on ourselves and our circumstances. This requires that we spend a lot of time 'in our head' thinking and wondering. Might it be a very practical thing that our Lord requires of us, to serve others? And in doing so He knows why we must do it – because it helps us heal as well as helps those we serve. Sometimes the directives that the Lord gives to us are in fact extremely practical. For example, Apostle Paul directs us more than once to "take captive" our

*Giving Back Will Give Back to You*

thinking, which we now know through science that taking captive your thinking and thinking on the good things that Paul lists actually changes your brain chemistry. So it is with giving to others even when you yourself are in need.

Giving back both gives to others and gives back to you. Giving back is much like throwing a boomerang. What you give out will come back to you. What you reap, you sow. Please note, the key in giving back is not to wait until you 'have it all together' and now your tough times are behind you. Instead, it's a matter of giving back and speaking hope into others' circumstances *even as you are going through* your tough times. As you help others even as you are needing help, it brings hope and healing to them, and it brings healing and hope to you. Why? Because in doing so you begin to see how the Lord is redeeming your pain and difficult circumstances, working them out together for your good. And how you give back actually helps, heals, and gives up to others! Suddenly you can begin to see the forest from the trees. You begin to understand what Scripture means when "we comfort others with the comfort that has been given to us." The Lord never lets any difficulty go to waste. He works it together for our good and then calls us to give to others to continue the healing He is working through our difficulties.

**Please take some time now and reflect on these few questions:**

Have you been giving back already? If not, do you believe that it might be an important thing for you to do? How might you go about giving back?

_____

_____

_____

_____

Think back in your life, have there been other difficult circumstances that you have gone through and then were able to help others because you yourself had experienced what they were going through? If so, how did that help you? How did that make you feel?

_____

_____

_____

_____

Take some time to list a couple of things that you believe you are learning and are areas where the Lord is working things out together for your good through your present circumstances of loving someone who has a mental illness.

_____

_____

_____

_____

Do you believe that the Lord wants you to give back to others? Do you believe that you have something to offer? What might be some of those things that you can offer as insights in loving someone who has a mental health struggle? What insights are you gaining in how to stay sane while you love someone who has a mental health struggle?

_____

_____

_____

_____

### *Prayer:*

*Lord Jesus, I find myself on a journey that is difficult. Many times, there is confusion, frustration, and worry that causes me to become hyper-focused on the circumstances I find myself, my loved one, and our family in on this journey. It just feels as though I need to "get through this difficult time" before I try to help anyone else. And yet You call me to comfort others with the comfort and insights I am learning even as I am going through things.*

*Forgive me for thinking I have to have it all together before I can help others! Forgive me for even thinking I can 'have it all together'! I forget that on this side of heaven, I will always be in process, always growing, changing, and going through one thing or another. So help me Lord, to move my eyes from being hyper-focused to looking for ways to give back to others so that Your healing and Your hope might flourish more in their lives and in mine.*

*In Jesus' name. Amen!*

## Chapter 11

# Resiliency in Suffering Which is Rooted in Hope

*Apostle Paul's Insights on Resiliency*

Joni Eareckson Tada, an evangelical Christian author, radio host, and founder of *Joni and Friends*, became a quadriplegic at age 17 after a diving accident. In her foreword to *Choosing Gratitude* by Nancy De Moss, Joni writes:

> Many decades in a wheelchair have taught me to not segregate my Savior from the suffering He allows, as though a broken neck — or in your case, a broken ankle, heart or home — merely 'happens' and then God shows up after the fact to wrestle something good out of it. No, the God of the Bible is bigger than that. Much bigger.
>
> And so is the capacity of your soul. Maybe this wheelchair felt like a horrible tragedy in the beginning, but I give God thanks *in* my wheelchair...I'm grateful *for* my quadriplegia. It's a bruising of a blessing. A gift wrapped in black. It's the shadowy companion that walks with me daily, pulling and pushing me into the arms of my Savior. And *that's* where the joy is.

Your "wheelchair," whatever it is – falls well within the overarching decrees of God. Your hardship and heartache come from His wise and kind hand and for that, you can be grateful. In it *and* for it.

When we experience extended situations that cause emotional suffering in our lives, it is extremely easy to become hopeless and we soon become battle weary. Chronic stress can wear you down both emotionally and even physically. Learning how to be resilient when ongoing difficulties 'hit' us in our lives is ever so important for long surviving, and growing in perseverance and character – which leads us to rock-solid hope.

Through the years of losing Donna's mom to suicide, Brad's two mental health episodes, Donna's cancer diagnosis, losing jobs, facing financial challenges, losing our dream home, and a whole lot of the challenges of life in general, we have grown in our resiliency when facing situations that cause suffering. It is what has held us strong through the various situations we have faced.

Chances are that you have probably been faced ongoing stress due to your loved one's mental health situation. Enduring it can be so draining, both emotionally and physically. You might be wondering how you are doing to be able to survive it. Well, we have found Paul's words in Romans 5:3-5 key in keeping us strong during extended situations of suffering we've gone through in our lives:

> *Not only so, but we also glory in our sufferings, because we know that suffering produces perseverance; perseverance, character; and character, hope. And hope does not put us to shame, because God's love has been poured out into our hearts through the Holy Spirit, who has been given to us.* Romans 5:3-5

Notice, Paul never imagined a Christian life without problems or trials. Peter, John, and all the first Christians were threatened and harmed. Paul was often persecuted. There was no such thing as a trouble-free Christian experience. And that is still true today. Unfortunately, within our modern Christian thinking there's a bit of heresy that has made its way into the Church. Many people in today's culture seem to believe that when we walk with the Lord this somehow wipes out suffering; that we shouldn't have to suffer if we love Jesus. Which simply is not true. In fact, the Lord tells us that in this life there will be many problems. He doesn't tell us that He will take those things away, but instead He promises to with us through them and even use them for our good.

When we are facing a situation of suffering in life, we must get our thinking straight! We suffer from the false thinking and idea that because we are Christians we shouldn't suffer. We also have some sort of western-world thought that we can overcome suffering, that we can alleviate it, or that we shouldn't have to suffer.

But we all experience some type of suffering due to our pain. Blogger Ken Cleary offers insight into what can happen in our attempt to manage that pain and suffering – we turn it into additional suffering by trying to provide relief:

> *'We all experience pain in our lives. Unfortunately, our attempts to manage pain often turn it into suffering instead of providing relief.*
>
> *Some common ways we create suffering include:*
>
> *Ignoring pain. When we ignore pain, we don't learn anything. Instead we often continually repeat the habits that create suffering.*
>
> *Making pain our story. When we turn pain into our default self-narrative, we can overlook the details of our emotions. We might*

*experience depression or anxiety as a solid, unchanging wall. But in reality the experience may be full of gaps and moments of freedom.*

*Rejecting our pain. Making an enemy of our experience can lead to suffering. When we push away our experiences and don't allow ourselves to explore and understand our feelings, we cannot learn or grow from them. Experience is just experience. Rejecting our thoughts and feelings is usually pointless. What's more, it can deepen the conflict in our lives. (Of course, some experiences may be simply too painful to examine for a time, or on your own. If you are dealing with something particularly difficult, please seek help from a qualified therapist or counselor.)'*

Excerpted from *Pain Is Inevitable; Suffering Is Optional* by Ker Cleary, March 30, 2010. GoodTherapy.org/blog/. Permission to reprint granted by GoodTherapy.org.

We have heard it said and have begun to believe, "What matters most is not what happens to you, but how you will use what happens to you." Paul most likely would have agreed. In these three verses, he's saying: You can become bitter and angry about hard and dark times, or you can see how God uses them to make you the Christian He always wanted you to be. Something good can come out of this. He summarizes how that happens using four key words.

## 1. Sufferings

This is the starting point. Paul does not discuss whether a Christian should experience sufferings; it's a given that the Christian will. There's no doubt and no debate. The Christian life is a hard life.

Our word *sufferings* translate the Greek *thlipsis*. At root that word means *pressure*. Pressure can destroy, but not always or necessarily. For example, there is a saying that tends to be the story of my life: "A deadline is the mother of motivation." The pressure of a deadline spurs me to work, and to word hard! One man describes how a heart attack was the best thing that ever happened to him. Why? Because, he said, for the first time ever he felt pressurized to exercise, and because he'd gone through the heart attack he'd taken up a disciplined exercise regime. And now he was strong and fit like he should have been all his life.

Please note: Paul is NOT saying that you and I should not feel and hurt during our suffering. In fact, he assumes that we will. Sometimes as Christians we assume toxic positivity. In other words, we 'suck it up', stuff down the emotions and feelings, and 'hang tuff' through all of it. But what happens to the feelings and emotions?

Paul is thinking like that, that good can come from suffering. In this one sentence he's not trying to give a full-blown philosophical or theological treatise on suffering. He's saying the sufferings that come from being a Christian generate good consequences in our lives.

**Good can come from suffering**

Paul goes on to list those good outcomes. What good can lie beyond sufferings?

## 2. Perseverance

"Suffering produces perseverance," Paul says.

If I ever enter a marathon it will prove the age of miracles is not past, or that I am completely insane. Trust me, it will not happen. I know some of the challenges marathon runners go through only because I have Googled it.

Many talk about 'hitting the wall', that moment when the body screams that it can go no further and it seems the race is over. One article in a running magazine called it "a bodily form of sedition" when the legs don't want to move, the stomach is erupting, and the brain begins to hallucinate. The body says 'stop'!

Oddly, a great number of marathon runners do manage to keep going, and often the pain begins to ease off. How can that happen? One theory is that a fatigued brain almost assumes the legs must be fatigued and could not run another step, so the brain shuts down the body. In other words, it's not the body that is saying 'stop', it's the brain. But – if that theory is right – there is strength left in the body, and if the runner can press on, new energy is found in those legs, and with determination that runner can finish strongly.

Suffering is real – Paul is in no doubt about that – but it doesn't mean the Christian race is over. Instead suffering spurs perseverance, the get-up-and-get-on instinct that carries someone through the trial and towards their goal.

## 3. Character

Paul goes on: "Suffering produces perseverance; perseverance, character."

If I said "Joanne is a woman of great character," I might be thinking she is a great example to others of how to live out the values with which she had been raised.

Paul probably uses the word character in a slightly different sense to my example. Paul is not thinking of the character someone *inherits* but the character they *become*. He uses the Greek word *dokimē*, and it means 'proven character,' the kind that comes from testing.

It's like precious metal put through white hot fire so that everything impure is burned away. Only the best remains.

The Old Testament character Job described that experience to his friends. Speaking about how God was dealing with him, he said: "But he knows the way that I take; when he has tested me, I will come forth as gold" (Job 23:10)

Job was experiencing great suffering, but knew it was the Refiner's fire, and he would come out as gold.

Suffering does not rob Christians of their potential. Suffering plus perseverance gets them to their potential. Christian character is not inherited, it's not taught, it doesn't even come through Bible study or prayer. Christian character comes through testing, walking the dark road of pain or hardship or persecution. What should not stay in our lives is burned away; what is needed for our lives grows stronger.

**4. Hope**

Paul writes: "Suffering produces perseverance; perseverance, character; and character, hope."

> **Hope keeps someone going against all odds**

Hope is what keeps someone going against all odds. Paul says it's suffering that produces perseverance, which in turn produces character, and out of that tested, refined character comes hope.

And – in closing these verses – Paul says, "Hope does not put us to shame." It doesn't disappoint. It's not vain hope, not hope without a reward.

We suffer but learn to persevere.

We persevere and through many trials and tests our character is formed.

Out of that godly character emerges hope – we look to God, we trust Him, we believe He has no plans other than good plans for our lives (Jeremiah 29:11), and we are not let down. We turned our eyes to heaven and were met by the tender eyes of the living God who pours His love upon us and into our hearts.

[Portions above used from *The Path to Hope* by Northern Seminary; May 13, 2013]

In his book *Hope Again: When Life Hurts and Dreams Fade* (1997, Thomas Nelson, pp xi-xii), Chuck Swindoll writes this about hope:

Hope is a wonderful gift from God, a source of strength and courage in the face of life's harshest trials.

- When we are trapped in a tunnel of misery, hope points to the light at the end of the tunnel. When we are overworked and exhausted, hope gives us a fresh energy.

- When we are discouraged, hope lifts our spirits.

- When we are tempted to quit, hope keeps us going.

- When we lose our way and confusion blurs the destination, hope dulls the edge of panic.

- When we struggle with a crippling disease or a lingering illness, hope helps us persevere beyond the pain.

- When we fear the worst, hope brings reminders that God is Still in control.

- When we must endure the consequences of bad decisions, hope fuels our recovery.

- When we find ourselves unemployed, hope tells us we still have a future.

- When we are forced to sit back and wait, hope gives us the patience to trust.

- When we feel rejected and abandoned, hope reminds us we're not alone … we'll make it.

- When we say our final farewell to someone we love, hope in the life beyond gets us through grief.

Put simply, when life hurts and dreams fade, nothing helps like hope!

## Devotional Reflection

*A bit of reflection:*

Why is it important to learn how to be resilient?

_____

_____

_____

_____

What stage of Romans 5:3-5 would define your current situation: suffering > perseverance > character > hope? What things can you do to move closer to hope?

___

___

___

___

***Prayer:***

*Heavenly Father, I know that you do not promise that a Christian's life will have no problems. But I'm feeling very overwhelmed right now. How can I find meaning or purpose in my sufferings when all I feel is stuck in them?*

*Forgive me for taking my eyes off You. I want to be a person of character. Help me to get my thinking straight. Open my eyes to understand and to do what's needed to move beyond the suffering phase. Please fill my family and me with the wisdom and desire to strive diligently to find hope and resiliency.*

*In Jesus' name. Amen.*

# Chapter 12

# Choosing Hope in the Face of Hopelessness

*In Christ, Hopelessness is a Feeling and Hope is a Reality*

Hopelessness is serious. Every day people fall into the hopeless hole of hopelessness due to their struggle with a mental health issue. Hopelessness begins to knock at the door of one's heart when you feel and believe that you have no future. It happens so easily, and it can take root all too fast. Each time we face one of life's interruptions which change our perceived future, hopelessness can settle in and live rent free in our hearts and minds.

(Brad) My manic episode was definitely a life-altering interruption. It resulted in me being asked to resign as pastor of one of the fastest growing churches in the denomination. It was earth-shattering. My position and the church had become my identity. I was devastated to the point of complete hopelessness. I had lost my future. Hopelessness had set in. And the deep dark hole of depression became a shameful guilt place of familiarity for me; months and months of severe depression followed.

For years prior to this interruption I had felt as though I had a monster inside of me that I had to manage. The more stress I experienced with pastoring a growing church, the more impossible it was to control the monster within me. So when I was diagnosed with bipolar disorder, I found out that the monster had a name. And strangely enough, a small ray of hope began to break through the hopelessness what had swallowed me whole.

Why would there be a small ray of hope following my diagnosis? After all, usually people see the diagnosis of bipolar disorder as the difficult thing to accept. Well, it was because people around me helped me see that the diagnosis and treatment of my bipolar disorder were a way back to having a future. The idea that the bipolar could be treated and I could have a future poked a small pinhole of hope into the darkness of hopelessness. It was not an easy journey, but it was more than worth it. With that small pinhole of hope, I could see a way forward. I began to grieve what I had lost, and began to embrace a new and different future; believing that I could live well in spite of having bipolar disorder.

At Brad's sickest and darkest time of the deepest point of hopelessness, he discovered something that carried him through. Many think it's difficult to explain hope and hopelessness, but we're going to take a very simple but clear view of the two and how, in fact, you can find hope in the midst of hopelessness.

Hopelessness, simply defined, is when you can't see a way forward. And who of us hasn't felt hopelessness, especially those with a diagnosis?

(Brad) I know when I was diagnosed with bipolar disorder, I thought, "Oh my gosh, the best is behind me. It's all over. There's no hope for the future. I can't go on." I felt very, very hopeless following a major episode in 1995. I felt so alone and so helpless in the midst of it all.

I had lost my way forward and hit a wall. I saw no way that I could go on, especially with all that had happened. So, I've been there. I know what I'm talking about. I've experienced it more than once. I've experienced it twice in my life where I'd been so hopeless that I was suicidal. Hopelessness is when you don't see that way forward.

So, what is hope? Hope is when you see a way forward – in spite of the circumstances that you're facing.

Hope and hopelessness are not complete opposites. It may sound kind of strange, that if you think you're hopeful, then you don't have hopelessness; and if you're hopeless, you certainly don't feel hope. But that's not been the way we have experienced it, and it's not what we see happens in Fresh Hope groups.

We believe hope is something that you and I have in Christ. We don't always have hope-filled situations on this earth, but we have this promise that God will always take every situation we go through and make it work for our good. Therefore, we have hope all the time. From our perspective, hope is a spiritual thing. It's a truth that sometimes we can't feel, sometimes we can't feel, but we have to hold onto with our faith, whether or not we feel it in that circumstance.

Hopelessness is something that you and I end up experiencing on earth. When our world became broken through Adam and Eve, hopelessness entered the picture. But we were never designed to be hopeless people. It hurts our brain chemistry, it hurts our souls, and it hurts our spirits to be hopeless. But it doesn't mean if I'm hopeless that hope is no longer there. That's why I say they're not opposites, nor are they mutually exclusive. You can feel hope at the same time you're feeling helpless. Hopelessness is something we experience on what I would call the horizontal aspect of life on earth – what we can see, feel, and experience from a human perspective, such as difficulties because of mental health disorders, loss of job, loss of spouse, or trauma that we've experienced as children or adults. Disasters can cause this kind of hopelessness. We question, "How do we go through this? What is the new way forward?"

Hope, on the other hand, is a vertical experience and truth. It comes from God. It was the way we were made. We were created to be hope-filled creatures, hope-filled human beings. In life, there are times where we live at the center point, where both hope and hopelessness intersect. Notice what image that creates: a cross.

If you're feeling hopeless, we want you to understand that you can still have hope even if you don't feel it. Know this, whether you feel it or not, you can in fact hold on to the real hope that comes from God.

Clinical research has been ongoing for over 25 years on how hope works. The findings give us strength and prove the evidence of what Brad experienced when he was at his worst. Dr. Sean Lopez's research (*Making Hope Happen*) supports what Brad experienced.

(Brad) When I thought I had no future, hopelessness set in and took over. But when I could see the way to a future, hope began to return. And the clearer the future became for me, the more hope I felt.

When you can begin to feel there's a way forward and that you can move beyond this point where you feel hopeless, that's when you begin to feel hope. Now you may not like the way forward because it may not be the same way you thought you were going to go. "Well, I don't know that that's really going to happen, but I can kind of see how I can get through this." But you can take it up another level by infusing that hope – that type of horizontal hope – and make it much better by infusing faith into that hope.

How is your 'hope tank' doing? Do you feel like you can see a way forward? If not, do you potentially need to let go of the future you thought would be, grieve it, and let it go? Do you need to embrace the new potential future? There's no doubt that doing this is a process. It is not like switching on a light switch. But, it is a choice.

> **How is your 'hope tank' doing?**

Hope is truly a choice. For us as Christians, hope is not only a choice, but it is sure and certain. Paul reminds us that no matter what our circumstances might be, there is a future because the Lord will work all things out together for our good (Romans 8:28). So, I certainly may not 'feel' hopeful, but I choose to believe Romans 8:28 and that means that there is a future. It may not have been the future I thought it would be, but it is a future.

What does that mean? That means that when we start looking at hope not from a horizontal perspective only, but also from this vertical perspective, we look at it through the promise of Romans 8:28, that God can work all things out together for good, for those who love Him and are called according to His plan and His purpose. Now hope has taken on a whole new meaning.

You may be aware that we live in Nebraska. If you know anything about Nebraska, you've heard of Big Red football and college football. With no professional football teams in our state, our focus is on our college team. And back in the day when they were winning championships, it was fun to watch them play and beat everybody. But if you follow college football now, you know that Nebraska has had some really rough years and gone through a number of coaches. But every time we get a new coach we think, "All right, we have hope. We have hope." That's this horizontal kind of hope. We hope we have a winning season. We hope we're going to be number one. Again, we hope... It's wishful thinking. Hope. It's good to have that. It helps you get through life.

We can have that on a horizontal level, but I'm telling you when you have a mental health issue and you don't see a way forward, and you don't even feel like you have wishful thinking kind of hope, that's when you need to infuse faith into it. And now with Romans 8:28, that no matter whether you win or lose the game, you're going to win – and it changes how you experience things.

Brad likes to think about it this way: I'm watching my Nebraska football game, and I'm hoping and wishing that they're going to win. But they're just playing terribly and it's horrible to watch the game. It's now halftime and they're behind. If I don't know how it ends or how it's going to come out, I'm going to watch the second half pretty intensely. I'm going to go through it differently than if I knew while I was watching that I was certain they're going to win. In that case, I'm going to enjoy every moment of it. Maybe not every moment, but I'm going to experience even the difficulties in the game differently because I know the outcome. And that's what it means to infuse faith into your hope. It means to think of it as you already know the ending. You already know what God can do with the hopeless points of your life.

As you experience it, yes, you may feel hopeless, but it does not mean that you are without hope. And this is important: you have to express that hopelessness. Here's where the Christian Church often does a number on us. Well-meaning people tell us, "Well, you just got to have more faith. You just got to pray more. You just got to trust God more." Blah, blah, blah, blah, blah, blah... And we say things like, "Don't feel that pain. Don't express your hopelessness. Don't..." as though it's not in the Bible. But it is. Look at the Old Testament. David's pretty desperate and hopeless in most of the Psalms. The truth is that amongst all of that hopelessness, David always comes back to the fact that from a vertical perspective, he has hope that gives him strength to endure the horizontal hopelessness that he at times has.

We get ourselves in trouble when we tell people, "Pray; trust God; there's always hope. There's never a hopeless situation," and not allow them to express their hopelessness. If you feel hopeless, it's okay. Express your hopelessness, but also know and choose to hold onto the truth that God will get you through this. There will be purpose in the pain. He will reuse it. He will reinvent it. He will redeem your pain.

Finding hope is not about a bunch of trite spiritual sayings. It's about a reality, a truth. It's about a vertical truth of God to man and man to God, but mostly God to man. It's God's assurance that there is always hope. It just happens to be that in this life, as we experience it, we have bouts of hopelessness. We have times where we're hopeless, but that does not mean we are without hope.

We discover hope in the midst of hopelessness, or actually we experience hopelessness in the midst of hope, because that's really what it is. From God's perspective, we have hope. It's eternal. 1 Corinthians 13 says, "Faith, hope, and love: now these three remain." Hope is one of the 'Big 3'. It's true now. It's true in the future. It's true for all time in eternity. Hope exists. Hope is there.

Everybody has some degree of hope. There's always hope. That's the truth. Sure, we have bouts of hopelessness in that truth. We experience it, and that's okay. The way God designed us is we can let that out. We express our hopelessness, and it may take days, weeks, it even months.

If you have a chemical imbalance in your brain, it's extremely difficult to choose anything except the lie that your brain is telling you – that you're in a hopeless situation. Because this is a chemical lie, it's imperative to be willing to have the doctor and other medical professionals help when there's a brain chemistry issue. If you shoot me up with methamphetamines in the middle of the night without me knowing, I'm not going to wake up being the same person. I'm not going to be who I am in my right mind. I'm going to have a difficult time navigating through life until that drug wears off. That's what happens when a brain is having chemistry issues. It's hard to be who you really are.

People will say, "Well, just choose. Think about it. Think about..." The truth is you are going to not be able to find hope as easily as when your brain's chemistry is balanced. The more straightened up the brain chemistry is, the more easily one can then choose hope by faith – faith-infused hope. It's important to get that brain chemistry straightened out. There's no shame in it. That's just the way it is.

If you love somebody who has a mental health disorder, it's so extremely important for you to hang in there with them. Allow and encourage them to express their feelings of hopelessness. This gives them hope in and of itself. Your goal is to help them to get their feelings out. Don't bypass their feelings, because that doesn't help. But also help them to realize that just because they believe life is hopeless, that doesn't make it true.

Hope can be borrowed, it can be shared, and it can be caught! Think about this: if you hang around a lot of hopeless friends, you will begin to feel hopeless.

And if you hang out with people who are filled with hope you will begin to feel hopeful. It's what all the research says. And when I don't feel hopeful, for instance, but somebody else has hope for my situation, even that can give me a little bit of hope. And especially when I feel that I'm being heard, I start to feel hope. What's crucial is that we *choose* hope *in spite* of what we feel.

Certainly situations occur on this side of heaven that bring about hopeless feelings. That's not unique just to those with mental health challenges. But when you are in Christ, no situation is truly hopeless. Jesus will make a way. He can and will. That's true. We know you may not feel it, you may not even want to hear it, but I (Brad) do know this, that that's what got me through. In the recesses of my mind, as sick as I was with the hopelessness, just feeling like it had swallowed me up and that there was absolutely no future, no hope for my life, I can honestly tell you that I felt like I was broken and beyond repair, that there was no way to go forward. And the only things that I could think of was how to get out of the pain. It was awful feeling that way, but in the deepest, darkest recesses of the little bit of right mind that I had inside of me, I knew that God would take it and make it work for my good.

> **Choose hope in spite of**

So I hung onto that for dear life. I fought. Sometimes you've got to fight so you get help to do everything again. You get your brain chemistry as straightened out as you can. You work alongside of the medicine and you keep choosing hope, and you keep the living out hope even if your feelings are the opposite.

Remember, the enemy always wants us to believe that it's all done. God's done with us. We're the exception. He lies to us, he deceives us, he makes us feel... All of those things play right into hopelessness, don't they? The reality is that God is *not* done with you, or the person you love, or the people you desire to help. God's not done. God can take it and turn it around for your good, make it work for your good.

So we ask again: how is your hope tank? Is your hope tank empty? Is being a caregiver sucking the hope right out of you? Do you see a way forward into the future? Are you strong enough to make the choice of hope? If not, we have hope you can borrow. We know, because of the storms we've been through in our lives, that God is at work in all things. He is with you. He has not left you, and He won't leave you. He is FOR you and your entire family! He has a plan. It may not be the life you planned prior to the interruption of mental illness, but *in spite of* it, He has a plan!

Everything may not be 'good' right now, but all is well because of Him. The Lord has heard every single one of your tears as a kind of 'liquid prayer'. Look for that little tiny bit of light coming through the pinhole poking through your hopelessness. Choose hope. Choose it minute-by-minute, hour-by-hour, day-by-day, and your feelings will begin to catch up. There is a future for you, and joy is included in it.

## *A bit of reflection:*

How did a small ray of hope break through for you when your loved one received a diagnosis?

_____

_____

_____

_____

Explain the analogy of the horizonal plane of hopelessness and the vertical plane of hope in Christ.

___

___

___

___

What is God's promise to each of us in Romans 8:28?

___

___

___

___

What does it mean to "find hope in the midst of hopelessness?

___

___

___

___

***Prayer:***

*O Christ, forgive my hopelessness. I know in my head that You promise to always be with me and fill me with hope, but my heart says differently.*

*I want to find a way forward. I need to find a way forward. Help me find hope once again.*

*I can't be of much help to my loved one if I myself don't have hope. Please forgive my lack of faith and trust in Your ability to provide hope and healing. Show me how to regain the joy that comes with sure and certain hope. Please send your Spirit to fill my hope tank and strengthen me in this journey.*

*In Jesus' name. Amen.*

# Part 2

# Helpful Hints

*For When Holding to Hope is Hard to Do*

# Part 2A
# Living Well

## Chapter 13

# Life is 10% What Happens to You and 90% How You React to It

(Brad)

A while back, Donna and I went to my 40th high school class reunion. I had not seen many of my classmates since Graduation. So you can imagine how strange it was to see them after so many years. Fortunately, our name tags included our senior class picture. Boy, was that helpful!

I found myself reflecting the entire evening how fast life goes and how no one's life necessarily turns out like they thought it would. When you have not seen someone for 40 years, you definitely can see the toll of living in their physical appearance. Of course, we all had aged (some better than others). And while our journeys have been very different, they share a common thread. That thread is made up of joy, happiness, disappointments, hurts, fears, brokenness, grief, hopes, mistakes, success, failures, dreams lived, and many dreams lost. I could see in my classmates' eyes that disappointments and brokenness had taken their toll. Living life can take the life out of you.

What's the point of this story? To remind you that life brings with it a lot of disappointments, pain, and brokenness. And life keeps on whether or not you are stuck in those things. I believe that we can easily get into a mindset that having a mental health challenge ruins your life and we think that we can't move forward in life or enjoy it. The truth is that everyone faces something in life. A mental health challenge is just one of the many obstacles found in this experience we call life.

It's so easy to begin to focus so much on ourselves and how 'hard' we have it that self-pity can start to creep in and take up residence in our beliefs. And while we're stuck in the pain and brokenness of the mental illness, life keeps going. But for me, life is way too short to get so stuck in self-pity or in believing that life is now 'over' because of a mental health diagnosis. Yes, a mental illness/disorder can suck. Yes, a mental health issue can hinder ones' life and alter the course of what we had hoped life to be. Yes, a mental illness is a 'cross to bear' in life. But lest we forget, many other crosses in life are just as difficult – and some even more – tragic and painful to bear. For me, it is imperative in keeping my self-pity at bay that I remember there are much worse crosses to bear in life than living with bipolar disorder.

I spent seven very long years stuck in my pain and brokenness following the manic episode that brought about the collapse of my life. Self-pity was a large part of that pain. I felt as though my life had been robbed from me. But it was really being stuck and feeling sorry for myself that was depriving me of life, not the bipolar disorder! And I didn't get unstuck until I got sick and tired of feeling sorry for myself and believing that my life was over.

I decided I was going to live well in spite of having bipolar disorder. Those three little words, 'in spite of' are the mantra of my recovery. To get unstuck I did three things:
- Changed how I was thinking by taking control of what I was thinking about. I did not allow myself to rehearse the pain and brokenness continually. Instead, I began to think about how the pain and brokenness could propel me into living well. (This was the hardest thing I had to do in recovery!)

- Set reasonable and reachable goals that continually moved me towards living life well. I stuck to the goals, and when reached, I set new ones. Yes, there were failures and setbacks. But I chose to see them as learning opportunities for living well.

- Started helping others with mental health challenges and moved my focus off myself. (This probably was the major game changer for me.) When I began focusing on helping others, I found my passion again; there was purpose for all of the pain I had experienced.

Here's what I know about life and how people live it, based not only on my life but also after pastoring for the past 30 plus years: everybody has stuff'. Everybody has pain. Everybody has tragedies and losses in their lives. Pain is pain. Whether it is the loss of a child, cancer, financial collapse, divorce, or a mental health challenge: you either work through it, or you get stuck in it. As they say, life is 10% what happens to you and 90% how you react to it.

**Set reasonable and reachable goals**

*A bit of reflection:*

How are you responding to the things that life is throwing you?

How are you reacting to having a mental health issue in your life?

Are you living well *in spite* of it? If not, why not?

# Chapter 14

# Wisdom for Living Well: Knowing the Difference Between What We Can Change and What We Can't Change

**Serenity Prayer**
by Reinhold Niebuhr (1892-1971)

God, give us grace to accept with serenity
the things that cannot be changed,
Courage to change the things
which should be changed,
and the Wisdom to distinguish
the one from the other.
Living one day at a time,
Enjoying one moment at a time,
Accepting hardship as a pathway to peace,
Taking, as Jesus did,
This sinful world as it is,
Not as I would have it,
Trusting that You will make all things right,
If I surrender to Your will,
So that I may be reasonably happy in this life,
And supremely happy with You forever in the next.
Amen.

These words from the *Serenity Prayer* by Reinhold Niebuhr have been key for us in learning how to live to well in spite of a mental health challenge: "The serenity to accept the things I cannot change; courage to change the things I can; and wisdom to know the difference."

(Brad) After being diagnosed with bipolar disorder I spent too much time focused on things I could not change, which led me to become frustrated, hurt, and angry. This side-trip on my road to wellness took me down a path that had the power to make me bitter and resentful. All this held me back from getting better. Thankfully, my therapist was able to help me get back on a path that led to wellness. The key was in knowing the difference between the things I could change and those things that I could not change.

*Some of the things I could not change:*

- I couldn't change other's reactions to my mental illness, including those close to me. (This was a big one for me!)
- I couldn't change the fact that I had (and still have) bipolar disorder and I couldn't 'will' it away.
- I couldn't change my past.
- I couldn't change the fact that I would need medicine.

This list could go on and on. The first point was a BIG one for me to accept and come to terms with: not being able to change people's reactions and opinions regarding my having bipolar disorder. I had lived my life doing a lot of 'people-pleasing', so it greatly mattered to me what other people thought and said about me. I wasted a lot of time and energy spinning my emotional wheels over this issue, despite that it was not something I could change nor was it was my responsibility. As I focused on the things I could not change, I found myself not changing the things I *could* change!

That which occupies your thinking is also the direction you go. As I obsessed on the things that I could not change, I became frustrated, angry and bitter about them. There certainly was neither serenity nor peace for me.

The previous paragraph and what follows applies also to you as a loved one. The key for us in accepting the things we can't change is to change our focus to the things that we can change.

As I focused on the things I *could* change, I began to get my life back. I know that whatever I focus on in my thinking is where I'm headed. I began to make a list of the things I could change and began to work on those things. It took a lot of willpower at first. I continue to choose to focus on the things I can change so that I might live well.

**Focus on the things that we can change**

*Some of the things I can change:*

- I can change how I respond to others in spite of how they have reacted to my disorder.

- I can find those who do understand and are supportive in spite of those who do not understand and not supportive.

- I can change learn from my past and take what I have learned and apply it to today and my future. I don't need to beat myself up over past mistakes.

- I can choose to live life well in spite of having a mental health challenge. In other words, my whole world is not wrapped in having a mental health challenge. It is just a part of my life, not the whole of it.

- I can change my doctor or therapist if they are not helpful.

I believe that knowing the difference between the things I can change and the things that I cannot change, and focusing on the things I can change, has been key to my living well in spite of having a mental health challenge.

*A bit of reflection:*

How about you? Have you or are you learning the difference? Are you focusing on the things that you can change and letting go of the things you can't?

What *can* you change?

What *can't* you change?

# Chapter 15

# We Are Not All the Same

It's essential to recognize loving a person with a mental health challenge is a different experience for each person. We are not all the same.

A mental health challenge differs from person to person. The same medicines do not work for all of us, nor do we all even have the same type of bipolar. The issues of mental health recovery are very complex. What has worked for me might not work for you. This is why we need one another.

When we connect, we empower each other to live well in spite of any possible daily battles with our disorder. Individually, no single one of us has all the answers. But together we have solutions for one another. Corporately we have answers for one another as we encourage each other and share what works for us as individuals in living well in spite of a mental health challenge.

**Together we have solutions for one another**

It concerns me when people talk about mental illness/health and over-generalize it, lumping everyone together. This shows the public doesn't begin to understand the complexities and challenges for individuals dealing with their particular life situations, plus having a mental illness.

Some have only one diagnosis, such as bipolar disorder, while others have the complexity of co-occurring disorders (also known as 'complex' disorders). Just having one mental health challenge in and of itself is enough to make life very complex. But add to that a borderline personality disorder, and now it's even more complicated. As we watch friends who have a personality disorder, lots of childhood trauma, and bipolar disorder, we have come to know that their struggle for wellness is compounded many times over as they strive to live well in spite of several mental health issues.

Yet we believe there are some general 'living-well' principles that are true for most, if not all of us. This list is not exhaustive, but include some of the principles that we believe may be universal to us all:

- In order to achieve some level of wellness in our lives, **we must be disciplined** to do those things that move us toward wellness and keep us well. This is a choice. As much as I hate to be disciplined, I choose to discipline myself daily to live well in spite of my mental health challenge.

- To live well, **we need other people** in our lives. You and I are made for community. Isolating will not help any of us to live well. If you have alienated all of the people in your life and are alone, then I strongly encourage you to seek out a Certified Peer Support Specialist, and/or a peer-led mental health support group or group therapy led by a professional therapist. You need other people.

- To live well, you and I **must be committed** to some of the hardest work we will ever do in our lives, whether you are the loved one or are the one living with a mental illness. It's a difficult job that sometimes must be done moment by moment, day by day. It's worth it.

- To live well, we must **have hope for our future**. If we lose hope, we will give up. Hopelessness comes about when someone believes they have no future. Choosing to believe that your life has purpose and meaning is key to overcoming hopelessness. If you are a person of faith, then this is where your conviction becomes key. Faith gives hope because it says that each life has meaning and purpose. Person of faith or not, your life is essential. Your life has meaning. Out of the pain and hurt of your life, you have the power to empower others just by telling your story. Telling your story to others who are also on this journey gives your life purpose. That's a future. And that gives hope. Never give up. Each of us needs you. You hold some answers for some of us in our journey towards wellness.

- To live well, we must **choose to look for the golden nuggets** in the 'poo-piles' of life. There's a lot of 'poo' in life. No one gets through life without pain and brokenness to varying degrees. When you and I let go of our expectations of life, it allows us to find the 'golden nuggets', the silver linings, even in the most difficult of times. Part of doing this means that we must never lose our sense of humor about how goofy life and others can be!

I believe these five principles are some of the foundational principles of a life of wellness. They are simple, so very important – and yet challenging at times to do.

## *A bit of reflection:*

Why is it important to include other people in our lives?

Which of the principles do you now or have you experienced with your loved one?

Which principles have you found to be most helpful in your loved one's path to wellness?

What additional things have you done and continue to do that help your loved one live well in spite of their mental health challenge?

## Chapter 16

# Medicine is Not a Magic Potion

Finding the right combination of medicines for those who have a mental health challenge can be more than just a little daunting. Many times, it takes a while to find the right medications and the right combination of medications that works for each person. Oh, that it would be so simple as to say everybody who has bipolar disorder takes this medicine or everyone who has depression takes this medicine, but it works so differently with people. Medicine interacts so differently that it is a journey in and of itself just to find the right medications. And then, with the side effects on medications, what we've seen through the years is so many people can't tolerate the medicine or they don't want to tolerate the side effects at all. Sometimes it's as simple as weight gain with the medication and they don't want to deal with that side effect. Or the side effects might go away within a period of time, and yet they're impatient and requesting the doctor to change the medication.

The struggle with finding the right meds is a very tough thing. In Brad's case, he has decided that he'd rather have weight gain than be insane, and Donna agreed. And while he struggles to lose weight because his medicine causes weight gain, that side effect is worth the benefits of being sane. Sometimes you can't have it all and you have to decide. The medicine helps him stay sane, but he has to work harder to lose the weight and is heavier than he would be without the medicine. In any case, medicine is a key component in helping your loved one get better, and it's necessary to find the right combination. Medicine and talk therapy together still prove to be the key medical parts of recovery that we need to help us get stable.

After the correct medicine is found and the brain chemistry is starting to straighten out, that medicine is still not a magic potion. Even when medication is working right, it isn't going to change their behaviors. It's not going to change their 'stinking thinking'. Your loved one may feel more positive, they may feel more like doing something, but they're still going to have to get up and change their thinking, and they're still going to have to get up and change what they do during the day. See, those of us who have a mental health diagnosis have to learn how to work *with* our medicine.

We have to do our part. We have to do our work. Our work is changing our habits. It's changing our negative thinking. It's learning new things. Looking at things differently. But, many of us just want a magic pill. If there was a magic pill that could take away the emotional baggage that people have, wouldn't that be something? If we could come up with that kind of medicine, we'd be filthy rich. But that kind of medicine doesn't exist. Instead, there's medicine that works with the brain, and helps the brain chemistry.

> **We have to do our part.
> We have to do our work.**

A doctor friend reminds us that it's called the 'practice' of medicine for a reason. Sometimes doctors don't know why the medicines work. And in the mental health field, that's true in regards to most of the medicines. So while your loved one needs medicine, you and your loved one need to understand that it's not a magic potion that's going to fix everything. They're going to have to work at recovering. The medicine is not going to cause their thinking to be different. It's not going to change the bad habits they may have developed during a long bout of depression.

A lot of people want to just take the medicine, but they don't want to do the work. Without doing the work, they can't reach their fullest potential. But sometimes folks get stuck here. They take the medicine, they're compliant with that, but that's it. That's kind of like finding out you have diabetes and you take the insulin but you don't really change your diet, you don't exercise, you don't do the other things that the doctors tell you to do. So you're only going to reach a partial fullness of your life.

People also get stuck here because, honestly, the work that those of us who have a mental health disorder have to do is hard work. It's consistently hard work, and it's proactive work, that we have to do.

After Brad's dad was diagnosed with bipolar, he consistently took lithium for years. But he never went to a therapist. He never worked through the emotional stuff from his childhood. He never worked through the baggage that he had from a long bout of depression. He was also diagnosed with diabetes, but never changed his diet. He just took the medicine.

A lot of people think that medicine is going to change it all, so they just take it and wait. It reminds us a lot of Christians who regularly go to church. They've got it, they believe. They go to church, but they never touch their Bible during the week. They don't pray at meals. They don't witness to others. They just go about living as they please, but they're in church on Sundays.

You get what we're trying to say? There's work to recovery. Your loved one is going to have to work with their medicine. They're going to have to change ways of thinking. They're going to have to change behaviors. They need to have the discipline of a daily routine, of going to bed at the same time every night and getting up the same time every morning, and not staying up all night. That's one of the very disruptive things that happens after people suffer from depression. When they start getting better, they still have this terrible sleep pattern, and a solid sleep regiment is absolutely necessary for any kind of mental health disorder because sleep allows the brain to reset and to rest. And your loved one is going to have to stay on the medicine while they're doing all this work. For sure, what happens to a lot of folks is they start feeling better and stop taking their medicine. Well, most likely, they're going to relapse. They've got to stay on the medicine and keep working with it.

*A bit of reflection:*

What struggles have you helped your loved one through in finding the right medicines?

What can you do to help your loved one understand that they must work alongside their medicines?

## Chapter 17

# Warning Signs of Potential Relapse

The potential for someone with a mental illness to relapse once they've begun to recover is a reality. Relapse many times happens after having been in recovery for some period of time. They think they're feeling so well that they don't need their medicine – and boom – they relapse. It happens.

Sometimes you can easily see the relapse, and other times it is so gradual it's hard to catch. So we want to just talk with you about some of the signs and things to look for regarding a potential relapse for your loved one.

First of all, you have to understand that medication can cause a relapse. The introduction of new medication into your loved one's system can cause an issue. Not taking medication as prescribed, or only taking it periodically when they want can cause an issue. Any kind of medication change, even as prescribed by the doctor, can trigger a relapse. It's imperative to watch carefully at any change of medication.

One of the things that we have seen over and over is people have little to no tolerance or patience for the side effects that come with medicine. Rather than hanging in there in spite of the side effects, patients will request their doctor change their medicine. Either they can't, aren't willing, or simply choose not to put up with the side effects. Whatever the reason, it seems when people can't settle into a medication, that relapses often happen. Many times the side effects subside, if they just wait it out.

In order for your loved one to avoid relapse, it is always best they take their medication as prescribed. To be completely compliant is the best remedy against relapsing. And any medication changes always need to be discussed first with the doctor.

You may be surprised to know that the use of substances like tobacco, caffeine, and sugar can cause or trigger a relapse. Substances can prevent certain medicines from working effectively, and can even make symptoms worse. So it's important to assess whether your loved one should stop using substances. Much research has been devoted to studying the effects of marijuana use in someone who has the propensity toward – or has – a mental health challenge, and has determined that marijuana greatly increases the risks of psychosis. Mind-altering substances such as marijuana really should be avoided at all costs, especially if someone is in their early twenties.

> **Substances like tobacco, caffeine, sugar, and marijuana can trigger a relapse**

Another thing that can trigger a relapse is when someone has too much stress and too many changes in their lives. Two kinds of stress exist: good stress and bad stress. Good stress is when we're excited about something we want, such as marriage, a job change, or moving to a new home. Bad stress is the stuff that you don't want to have happen, maybe a loss of some kind. Both kinds of stress can trigger a relapse.

So when looking for symptoms of relapse, too many life changes can be significant. If your loved one is avoiding the stress-causing issues they need to process, that avoidance can trigger a relapse. Resiliency is the ability to cope with problems and

*Warning Signs of Potential Relapse*

stress, to work through them, to not avoid them, but also to not create too many of them in one's own life. That's the goal.

In addition, physical issues can cause a relapse. If your loved one has chronic pain or a physical disability, or ongoing frustrations with their physical health, it can cause a relapse. For instance, even having surgery could potentially cause a relapse.

When you see a loved one's self-care deteriorating, it's often a sign that relapse is happening. Typical signs include if your loved one stops showering, doesn't care for themselves, doesn't want to change their clothes, or they don't want to get out of bed.

In some ways, you could look at relapse and the warning signs of potential relapse as if seeing their original symptoms recur. Symptoms that were first there prior to the diagnosis return, or the symptoms get worse. It's important to see the warning signs, because recognizing the warning signs gives you and your loved one a chance to take action before the illness takes control again.

You want to help your loved one learn how to avoid relapse, and you need to do that when they're doing well, not when they're relapsing. Do it when they're living well and they've got a handle on their recovery. Talk with them about it. Discuss "How do we avoid this? How do we work through it so that we don't have to go through this again?"

Now again, with everything said, sometimes the brain just messes up, and it has nothing to do with what your loved one has or hasn't done, or what has or hasn't happened in their life. But more times than not, it's because of one of those things that relapse happens. So developing a Wellness Plan is so important.

You can download and post a Wellness Recovery Action Plan (WRAP), an extremely detailed plan of prevention for relapse, through the FreshHope.us site, or directly at mentalhealthrecovery.com/wrap-is/. Also, we've discovered that the Eli Lilly Company has developed Team Solutions and Solutions for Wellness that contains a tool called *Recognizing and Responding to Relapse*. It's extremely good and can be downloaded from the internet.

*A bit of reflection:*

In what ways can medicine cause a relapse?

What is the best thing your loved one can do to prevent relapse?

What types of substances can contribute to a relapse?

How can a WRAP help avoid relapse?

## Chapter 18

# Perfection vs. Imperfect Progress

(Brad)

While waiting to weigh in at a Weight Watchers meeting many years ago, the woman in front of me stepped on the scale and began to cry. The leader, who was the person weighing her in, asked her why she was crying. Between her sobbing and trying to catch her breath, she said that she hadn't had a good week. When asked why, she replied that she had eaten some peanut M&Ms. The leader then asked her a very important question: 'Did you eat as many as you would have consumed before coming to our group?' And the woman, between her tears and sobbing, chuckled and said, 'Ohhhh NO! I ate only a small bag of them. Before group, I would have devoured a huge family-size bag!' The leader simply looked at her and said, 'Good for you! See? That's progress!'

The memory of that lady weighing in has been forever etched in my mind. It was at that moment I learned a life lesson about recovery: recovery is not about perfection; rather, it is about imperfect progress.

If you're like me, when you and/or your loved one are triggered by a situation and step back into old patterns or ways, you can easily believe that you have failed at recovery. It feels like someone unleashed the Hoover Dam of guilt, shame, anger, sadness, confusion, hurt, and being a total failure. But the truth is that you are not a total failure. If you recognize what's happening and learn from it, this is actually 'imperfect progress'. It's only failure if you don't acknowledge or learn from it, or if you decide not to return to working your recovery and instead remain stuck there.

This journey of wellness is not one of perfection. It is a journey of imperfect progress. To make this journey both you and your loved one must be willing to accept the fact that none of us are perfect, and are never going to be perfect. Recovery, which we define as taking back one's life in a new way, is built upon failures in which we learn from, get back up, and continue to move forward. Shaming ourselves and believing that one failure constitutes us as complete failures simply is a lie straight from the pits of hell! Everybody fails. Everyone falls short of the mark. What makes the difference between those who decide to give up and believe the lie that they are total failures, vs. those who succeed? It's simple: understanding that moving forward is one of imperfect progress vs. perfection.

Note: No matter how long your loved one might have been stuck believing the lie that they will never be able to change or move forward, it's not too late to help them get back up, dust themselves off, learn from what has happened, and begin to move forward. It is NEVER too late. When getting back up, it is important for them to take full responsibility for their issues, make amends if necessary, and decide to learn from it.

**It is never too late**

When failures involve a loved one, it can be difficult to get out of the stuck spot of believing the lie of never being able to move forward when the other person doesn't let it go. This type of situation is very challenging. When they are 'stuck' and won't let go of the past, it is at that point that you have to know that you've done what you can about the past (reconciling, taking responsibility, apologizing, asking for forgiveness, etc.), and you need to recognize that it is no longer your issue; it is theirs. We're learning that when this happens within our relationships, we absolutely must give a loving response to their reminders of the past, instead of getting triggered and repeating the same things over and over.

I want to encourage both you and your loved one. You are not a failure. Yes, sometimes you fail; so does everyone else. But failing does not make you a failure. Failing is a sign of moving forward and learning from it. Wellness does not require perfection at all. It is made up of imperfect progress that is simply handling one's failures in a healthy and appropriate way.

## *A bit of reflection:*

Complete this phrase: "Recovery is not about perfection; rather, it is about _____ _____.

According to Pastor Brad, what is 'imperfect progress'? How would you apply this to your journey with your loved one?

Failing does not make you a failure. What does failing actually indicate?

Have you had times when you've wanted to give up because you 'slipped up' in helping your loved one, or want to give up because this journey of wellness is hard work? What are you learning from your imperfect progress?

# Part 2B
# Relationships

# Chapter 19

# What Empowers Your Loved One Vs. What Enables Them

This can sometimes be a real balancing act, as we talked about in Chapter 6 with the illustration of the teeter-totter.

What does enabling look like?

- You are more willing to do the work of recovery than they are
- You soften the blow of their decisions to the point where they don't feel the sting of hitting bottom
- You make excuses and cover for them
- You ignore their issues, or deny they exist
- You don't hold them accountable
- You fear that what you say or do may cause a blow up or trigger your loved one
- You hold in your hurt and wounds out of fear
- You put all of your loved one's needs before your own
- You have difficulties expressing your emotions…or don't even know what you are feeling because you have ignored or stuffed them for so long
- When you begin to feel resentment toward your loved one

What are some signs that you most likely are enabling your loved one? When you find yourself wanting your loved one's recovery more than they want it, and when you find yourself more willing to do their work within recovery. (Yes, of course, there are times that they are not well enough to do some of the things that may be necessary for recovery, like finding a doctor, etc. But there is a time that they must own their recovery, and decide they really want to work it.)

Please note, sometimes those with a mental health diagnosis have been rescued or kept from the pain of the illness, and this keeps them from getting better. Sometimes we have to reach bottom or feel the pain, because that moves us to decide to do the work of recovery. The truth is, people usually choose to get better **when the pain of getting better is less than the pain of staying sick**.

There's a difference between enabling someone versus empowering them. Empowering means that you care and help with clear boundaries and accountability.

Not enabling someone – vs. empowering them – is tricky. To empower involves giving them a 'hand' in something that they are unable to do themselves. Yet excessive empowering in unhealthy ways actually perpetuates the problem, and can even create new problems. All too easily our love, care, and fear for our loved one can become control – and not help.

**Enabling vs. empowering is tricky**

*Good Therapy.org offices this insight about enabling:*

> *'Enabling is a distorted attempt to solve problems. Enablers desperately desire to find a solution to the issues at hand, but their attempts to do so are severely limited by the dysfunctional family system.*

*Enablers frequently find themselves thinking things like:*

- *'If only I can keep this person going through their current crisis, it will buy us another day.'*
- *'If I can't change what they've done, at least I can help limit the damage of that choice.'*
- *'Maybe my loved one will wake up and come to his or her senses. Maybe a real solution is waiting right around the next corner.'*

*Enabling has the effect of releasing the enabled person from having to take responsibility for his or her behavior. Enabling means that someone else will always fix, solve, or make the consequences go away. When someone is in the throes of an addiction or other grossly dysfunctional behavior pattern, he or she begins to rely on the resources available. Enabled persons will come to expect that their behaviors are disconnected from consequences or negative outcomes. Enabled persons may even begin to hold their enabling family members in 'emotional hostage' in order to keep this pattern going. They may learn to manipulate their enablers in order to ensure that the help and support keep coming.*

*In this kind of a system, everybody loses by inches. The enabler is desperate to prevent one enormous crisis, but winds up experiencing a constant state of stress as he or she attempts to manage each smaller daily crisis. Enablers generally are aware that they are being taken advantage of in some way; they often report feeling frustrated, unappreciated, and resentful.*

*The enabled person becomes stuck in a role in which he or she feels incompetent, incapable, disempowered, dependent, and ineffectual. He or she may gradually accept a self-concept that includes these negative traits, destroying self-esteem.*

*How, then, does the enabled person also "lose"? The enabled person may wish he or she felt in control of themselves, particularly with regard to addiction; but lacking the life experience and lessons that facing consequences brings, they may not know how to break those patterns. They may not have had the benefit of true self-reflection and self-evaluation of their behaviors. The enabled person becomes stuck in a role in which he or she feels incompetent, incapable, disempowered, dependent, and ineffectual. He or she may gradually accept a self-concept that includes these negative traits, destroying self-esteem and rendering the person even less likely to suddenly do a 180 and become responsible and self-sufficient in the future. The enabled person may essentially be prevented from building the skills and motivation he or she needs in order to practice responsibility and reach his or her full potential. Because the enabler(s) will always solve problems for them, the enabled person does not learn how to solve their problems themselves.*

*By this point, you may be thinking, 'I can see some of the ways I have been enabling my loved one. What now?'*

*You must accept that while your enabling behaviors come from a place of love, enabling is an ineffective way of solving problems at best; debilitating to all involved at worst. You may buy another day or prevent another emergency, but in the end, you are only postponing the real solution.'*

## What Empowers Your Loved One Vs. What Enables Them

Excerpted from *Enabling 101: How Love Becomes Fear and Help Becomes Control* by Kyle S. King, October 18, 2013. You can read the complete blog at GoodTherapy.org/blog/. Permission to reprint granted by GoodTherapy.org.

### How to Stop Enabling

When you love someone with a mental illness, all too easily you can begin to enable them to stay sick or not get completely well. The love you have for them and the desire to help them can easily become fear and control. So, how do you keep from enabling them, while helping and loving them at the same time?

*Here are some suggestions on how to stop enabling:*

- First, **accept that you can't fix them**. You are extremely important and can help them along in their recovery, but you can't make them recover, nor can you make them 'do' their recovery. That is out of your control. Recognizing this is key in keeping you sane as you walk alongside your loved one on this journey.

- **Only help them with what is absolutely necessary**. And when they succeed at something, cheer them on loudly!

- **Set concrete boundaries and consequences**, and stick to them. This helps both you and your loved one. It provides sanity in the craziness of a mental health challenge.

- **Let your loved one see and feel the consequences of their behaviors.** If you soften the blow all the time, it doesn't allow them to feel the brunt of their choices (or even the lack of making a choice). Remember, people don't usually get better until the pain of staying sick is more than the pain of getting better.

- **Only talk with them about the issues that you need to bring to them when they are having a lucid, 'more present', day or moment.** Don't try to address issues when they are not doing well. (Donna) Trying to reason or disagree with Brad when he was manic (prior to his treatment for bipolar disorder) was like standing in front an 18-wheeler coming right at me. I might try to point out that he's 'off', but all I received was vehement denial. So I had to pick the best time to confront and discuss matters – and even that was a risk. The 18-wheeler could appear at any moment.

- **Take care of your own responsibilities,** and care for yourself and others in your family. You need to take control (what you can – not what you can't – control) of your own life and the things you want to do.

- **Manage your anxiety and fears about your loved one and the situation.** You don't want your anxiety and fear to drive you to control your loved one. This will complicate things and potentially drag out the recovery even longer, as your controlling them becomes an issue for them that they resent.

- **Attend a Mental Health support group** for yourself, where your loved one can go along or not. For instance, with Fresh Hope groups, we have both the loved ones and those with a diagnosis in the same group. You are also welcome to attend even if your loved one does not attend. And if you can't find a local Fresh Hope group, attend an online group.

- Don't hesitate to **seek out professional help**. Talking with someone who is trained and licensed can benefit you greatly in keeping your own sanity throughout the journey to wellness.

To help, but not enable, your loved one will give them the opportunity to get better, sooner than later, if they so choose to take on their own recovery process and begin to live well in spite of their own mental health challenge.

## *A bit of reflection:*

What are the signs that you are enabling your loved one?

How do you enable your loved one?

How does empowering differ from enabling your loved one?

What can you do this week that will stop enabling your loved one?

## Chapter 20

# Creative 'Non-Confrontive' Ways to Confront Your Loved One

As you may know already, it can be ever so challenging at times to address any issues regarding your loved one's mental health. For them, they may or may not see it that way or may not even remember what you might attempt to address. Sometimes due to the mental illness, their reality is altered. Because of their brain chemistry issues, their experiences, feelings, perceptions, and insights are not based upon the shared reality of those around them. These sorts of things then make it so difficult to ever address issues with them. All of this will cause your loved one to become dismissive or defensive when you attempt to address any problems regarding their mental health and behavior. So, how might you creatively "confront" (address) your loved one in a non-confrontive way?

*Here are a few ideas:*

- **Don't assume** you know what is going on for your loved one. Ask questions such as, "How can I be supportive?" "How are you feeling?" "Can you help me understand?"

- **Be patient** with your loved one and yourself. This a process for everyone, and it takes time. There are no straight paths.

- **Educate yourself** – learn all you can about your loved one's diagnosis. This will help your loved one see that you care. It will also give you insight into what is going on for your loved one that they cannot articulate. *(NAMI provides great educational classes for family members; this can be a great way to gain correct insights and understanding. Plus, you meet other family members who can also share insights and creative approaches that have worked for them.)*

- **Use rules that were created for the whole family**. No one in this house will tolerate this behavior.

This approach may seem extreme, so here's an example: if your loved one is a young adult, someone who is dependent yet is defiant about taking their medicine, as a parent you might create a 'rule' or norm that says, *"I love you, and because I love you, I want what is best for you. And what is best for you is to take your medicine regularly as prescribed. So, we want to make an agreement with you that as long as you are living here with us, you take your medicine as prescribed. If you're not able to do that, then we have to address whether or not you are going to be able to live here."*

**Learn all that you can**

Before addressing any specific issues, it's always best to use this 'rules approach' if the family or household has come together and created the "rules" together, with buy-in with the dependents living in the home. And all need to understand that if someone does not adhere to the household 'rules', there have to be consequences. This, of course, is extremely difficult when your loved one is defiantly dependent. If you use this approach, we believe it's essential for both parents to agree on it ahead of time, along with input from your loved one's doctor and therapist, before approaching them.

- **See a counselor** for yourself. Seek answers for your questions. Sometimes our own issues can cause difficulties in our relationship with our loved one. Remember, we all have our issues. And if your own issues are causing complexities and additional problems within your relationship with your loved one, then working on your problems will be an added benefit in improving your relationship with your loved one.

Seeing a counselor for yourself can also be a place for you to work through your resentment, hurts, and emotional pain caused by your loved one's mental health challenges. It can also be a safe place for you to work through and address any anxiety you might feel and what might be happening for you emotionally regarding your loved one's mental illness.

- **Seek others** who are going through the same kind of situation. Healthy support groups can provide you with the opportunity to meet others who are or have been in similar situations and may provide you with new insights and creative approaches. For example, in the second half of our Fresh Hope support group meetings, we offer the loved ones time to meet as their own small group. This small group time is an excellent opportunity for loved ones to ask questions that will lead to the other loved ones sharing insights and creative solutions that have worked with their loved ones.

  However, within the first half of each meeting, both the loved ones (family and friends) and those who have a diagnosis meet together in a big group. This is an excellent time to gain insights and creative approaches from participants who have a mental health diagnosis. For example, the parent of a defiantly dependent offspring can often gain great insights into how to approach their loved one from someone who has a mental health diagnosis who was defiant and non-compliant in the past.

- **Don't Be Discouraged** when you don't handle it right. Remember, everyone is learning how to live in this unwanted reality. You will make mistakes. Remember, there are no perfect people. Simply determine to learn something from every mistake you make as you journey through this together with your loved one.

We offer these approaches to get you thinking about how you might approach your loved ones about things that could easily cause them to become defensive. Remember, these are just a few ideas. By joining a healthy support group such as a Fresh Hope group or by attending a NAMI Family to Family class, you can gain so many insights and creative approaches from others who are your peers (those who are going or have gone through the same thing). In support groups that are healthy and helpful, we have seen the Lord connect people in ways that only He can do. And in that connection, He provides ideas, insights, course-corrections, answered questions, peace, and hope that can be found in bearing one another's burdens. When we share each other burdens within a support group setting, it truly is a holy experience.

## *A bit of reflection:*

With well-meaning intentions, identify at least one situation where you confronted your loved one and it resulted in defiance or defensiveness?

Which of the ideas above could you realistically apply to 'creatively' confront that same concern?

# Chapter 21

# When You Are the Spouse

(Donna) What does it mean to be the spouse of someone with a mental illness?

Confusing; scary; devastating; terrifying; hurtful; experiencing a life-altering loss; feeling alone, forgotten, grief, anguish, and distrust; being fearful and overwhelmed.

In 1995, Brad was displaying what we now know was uncontrolled manic behavior. He would go away for 3 days and write sermons for the entire year. He saw himself working harder than anyone else, and was frustrated by others taking longer to complete tasks than he thought they should. He became so very angry, and we started having horrible fights. At this point, I was already worn out from the events of the previous year. Just days prior to my birthday, my father had died of cancer, 5 years to the day that my mom had taken her life. My grief was intense. I couldn't eat, and when I did, I had digestive issues. I was terrified of the future. How were we going to make it financially? Would Brad be able to work again?

> **We are encouragers, counselors, referees, mediators, and guards**

Sound familiar? On top of all of these feelings we are expected to keep everything going and help our spouse with this disease.

We do it a minute at a time, as we learn. We are encouragers, counselors, and referees. We are mediators and guards. When our loved one has high or lows, we set aside our own hopes and dreams to help them get back on track. We fight with them, for them – when they don't even know. We know and experience the devastation of ruined relationships, yet we want to protect them because we understand that it was not their intent, and in normal circumstances it would not happen.

I was the Preschool teacher at the church when Brad had his manic episode. I finished up the term, thinking I would return in the fall. But after the extent of the situation hit me, I knew I couldn't return. I wouldn't make it through the days knowing that I was not wanted.

Many days I would sit in our backyard and weep (while Brad was in the house doing the same). I would plead with God, 'My husband is not well. I have no job. I've got two children to care for. What am I going to do?'

It's hard as a loved one, because you get treated the same as if you are the one with the disease. Our daughter's peers gave her a very hard time and caused her a great deal of hurt. I found the Christian community to be sorely lacking. Very little compassion was shown to us, and even less after Brad's relapse seven years later. I was still the worship leader, but I cried every Sunday as I had to face the people.

We don't always tell our loved one what has been said or done to us, because we want to protect them. We experience rejection, ridicule, and grief because of their behavior. Yet we also know that if they could be in control, this would not be happening. We struggle with all of these feelings and work hard on not being resentful. We deal with fears of being able to trust, yet we do. We are at times overwhelmed. It's enough to cause us to have mental health issues ourselves.

So how do we carry on? We learn about their disease. We make mistakes and try again. We go to counseling and learn how to best help them. We make changes in our lives to accommodate their needs.

Can we do this? Some days better than others.

Why would we do this? Because we love them. We know that mental health issues are treatable if our spouses take their medicine.

We believe in the person we know them to be when their disease is not controlling them. Because we have learned that the very thing that draws us to our loved one is also the very thing that has brought devastation to our lives.

It all begins with love. We do it because we love them.

What do we need? (Make these known to your loved ones.)

- Patience. We are human, and we will not always handle everything perfectly
- For them to take their medicine and to keep their doctor's appointments
- Their trust in us when we question their behavior
- To know that we do this because we love them, but some days we are totally worn out from the dance we have to do
- To remember that it's not all about them.
- Friends to lean on when the road gets tough
- Most of all, to handle such a sometimes-difficult way of life, we need the strength and wisdom that come only from God

There are certain things that as a spouse you will always deal with. It's just part of the territory. God is faithful, and if you let Him, He will get you through.

Now we can say, 20 years after the first diagnosis, these words:

**Relief**

**Light**

**Laughter**

**Joy**

**Future**

**and Hope.**

*A bit of reflection:*

What barriers and frustrations have you experienced with your spouse?

What have you learned in traveling the road to recovery with your loved one?

Which needs would you list as most important for you to receive at this time?

## Chapter 22

# Learning to Trust Again

In a Fresh Hope video we made some years ago in which Amy Simpson, best-selling author of *Troubled Minds*, said, "Mental illness is defined as a disorder of some kind that affects your ability to think normally, feel normally, or process life's experiences normally. All of which affects one's behaviors and choices. Behaviors and choices that one makes when the brain is working properly are going to be quite different than when the brain is not working properly. That's why it is called "behavioral health." When someone has a mental illness, poor choices and inappropriate behavior become the symptoms of the mental illness. And while that does not excuse hurtful and inappropriate behaviors, it certainly does explain them.

(Brad) When I was out of mind, I was not in control of myself at all. And there were times, too many times, that I didn't even recall what I did, why I did it, or even where I had been. Other times I was aware of my behavior but could not stop myself from acting upon impulses that would not have been a problem when in my right mind. That's what my own brain was doing to me when my bipolar disorder was not treated. It's a horrible experience. Yes, the elevated mood was a good feeling, but then the high got way too high, and my behaviors became more and more bizarre – at least the bits I remember. My bipolar disorder is not an excuse for my behaviors; it is the explanation of why my behaviors were so bizarre and out of character for me.

(Donna) When his bipolar disorder was at its worst, Brad's behaviors caused him to do many hurtful things, and my trust was broken in significant ways. Following his major manic episode in 1995, while it was not easy finding out that Brad had bipolar disorder, many things began to make sense. Understanding some of the hurtful behaviors and painful things he said helped me be able to separate which of his behaviors were due to simple choice, and which behaviors came about due to the mania of the bipolar disorder. Again, not an excuse, but the explanation, the understanding. I knew Brad before the bipolar disorder 'took over'.

Following his initial diagnosis, I told Brad, "I know who you are, and this illness has caused you to behave contrary to that. Because I know your heart, I'm willing to stay and do this together – as long as you do everything within your power to maintain your mental health and not allow the bipolar disorder to rule over you." Trust had been broken. And this was possibly the first step that I took to begin to trust my husband again, understanding the difference between who he was and what behaviors and issues the bipolar disorder was causing.

Your loved one's mental illness/disorder may have caused behaviors that have broken trust. So, we have some ways to begin to trust again:
- **Forgiveness:** It's not possible to move forward without forgiveness. If your loved one is in recovery, doing what is necessary for their mental health, a crucial part for them will be to be able to move forward. Forgiveness is

good for everyone; yourself included, as unforgiveness puts yourself in spiritual jeopardy. And while forgiveness is a process, it is also a choice. In forgiving, there is a way forward. Without forgiveness, one remains stuck in the past. Forgiving, and the ability to move forward into the future, for both of you must happen before you can begin to trust again.

- **Trust Yourself:** Ask questions, talk about your concerns with your loved one and others. Educate yourself about the illness. Was trust broken due to the mental illness? Is it necessary for your loved one to be in recovery and take responsibility for the past and their future in order for you to be able to trust them again?

> **It's not possible to move forward without forgiveness**

- **An Accountability Group:** A group of peers (*others just like yourself, who love someone with a mental health challenge and have lived the experience*) to help you keep things clear and honest. You don't have to do this on your own.

- **Set Boundaries:** After Brad's major manic episode in 1995, Donna laid out three things that I could not live with. These were my boundaries. These three things gave him clarity as to what I expected. These three things also gave me clarity as to what I needed to remember as my bottom line. Please note, you have to make sure you can follow through on set boundaries. If you set boundaries and then don't keep them, that does not help your loved one or yourself.

- **Fears:** Explore your fears – why, what, how, letting go, moving forward. A counselor can help.

- **Faith:** It is a step of faith to let go of control for the other person. This doesn't mean you won't have concerns. Trust is really built when you begin to let go. Mutual boundaries can be set here to give some sense of peace as you expand. The first time Brad went out of town by himself after his major manic episode was very difficult for Donna. But gradually, each time got easier. Trust was being renewed.

- **Letting go:** Moving forward to a new reality. You don't forget, but you let go of the feelings and move to a new beginning, now more educated and more aware.

*A bit of reflection:*

Complete this statement: "Poor choices and inappropriate behavior become the symptoms of _____ _____". How can you apply this to your situation?

Why is it not possible to move forward without forgiveness?

Identify what boundary/boundaries you need to set with your loved one.

## Chapter 23

# When Children Are Involved

When a parent has a mental health crisis, it affects everyone in the home. It can be difficult for everyone to navigate through a territory they know little-to-nothing about, especially for children. When we lost Donna's mom to suicide, our children were 2 and 6 years old. One of our first questions was, 'What do we tell the kids?' Of course, we needed to tell them that she had died. But what if they asked how she died? We sought out advice, and came to the conclusion that secrets kept in a family are not good. As they say, we are as sick as our secrets. We told the kids that she died. But we waited to share any details until they asked, and the extent of our response depended on their age and ability to understand.

When our lives were struck by Brad's manic episode and mental health diagnosis in 1995, our children were 9 and 13. Not only was the episode very painful and entirely disruptive for our family, but it was so very public, which added some complexities concerning how much and what to tell the children. This fell squarely on Donna's shoulders at the time. So, we have a tender spot in our hearts when children are involved, because we know that their experience with the mental health crisis of one of their parents, and what they know about it, has a lasting effect upon them that they carry into adulthood.

What to tell children vs. what not to tell them can be a challenge, especially if it is their parent who is sick and you're the parent who has to handle how much to tell. You might find it helpful to think of it this way: what would you do if it were cancer or some other life-altering physical illness?

If you have children spanning a wide range of ages, how much and what you share will vary according to their ability to understand the situation. You might start by gathering them together and sharing minimal information based on the comprehension level of the youngest child, and then encourage them each to come to you on their own and ask questions.

Sometimes this can be very difficult, especially when a serious suicide attempt has occurred and your child was a witness. In this situation, we strongly suggest you should seek the advice of a professional therapist. And in most cases it will be most helpful for all of your children to receive counseling on an ongoing basis.

It's important to understand that just because a parent has a mental illness, it does not mean that their children will. The offspring may or may not have a propensity to having a mental health issue. Ask your doctors what can be done to help your child/ren from developing anxiety and stress. Proactive preventive care is especially important, because it will give them the tools to deal with stress and thereby avoid the perfect storm within their own mental health. As a parent of young children, you'll need to do this for them. But as they grow you can teach and equip them to use the tools by themselves.

**Proactive preventive care is especially important**

*Here's a starting list of things that we offer to you if children are involved in the mental health challenge that your loved one and you are facing:*

- **Knowledge of the diagnosis**: Help them understand the mental health diagnosis with age-appropriate information.

- **Room to express feelings**: Allow them to express their feelings.

- **Let others help**: A trusted friend, relative, or counselor can provide a safe place for them to express their feelings. Sometimes kids are concerned that if they share their feelings with their parents, they will hurt their parents' feelings. So a trusted friend can many times be that 'go-to' person for them.

- **Keep daily routines** as much as possible.

- **Communicate**: Keep the children informed on what is happening. Depending on the age, give them age-appropriate information.

- **Create New Memories**: Do some fun things. Don't live in the stress of the situation constantly.

- **Listen, listen, listen**: They need to know you hear their needs.

- **Be present:** You can't fix everything, but you can be available for them in the moment.

- **Visit Someone Special:** if things are really disrupted in the home, send the children to spend a little time with a grandparent, or someone else they can visit that is a real treat for them.

- **See a counselor:** It can be helpful for the children to be able to talk to a therapist who specializes in children, especially when there has been a significant mental health crisis such as hospitalization, a suicide attempt, etc.

As a parent who is caring for the one who has a mental health issue and caring for the children, it's a heavy burden to bear. But do the best that you can do, and count on the Lord bringing about what you cannot do. Children are resilient. They do best with age-appropriate truth at the right time. Family secrets hold power and can be very hurtful. And remember, you don't need to do this alone. It's OK to lean on a trusted friend, a counselor, family member(s), or all of them!

It might help you to know that our two children are now grown adults with their own families. They are well adjusted and emotionally mature despite our failures... lol! We each have a beautiful and healthy relationship with each of them. We believe that the Lord has used what they went through as children for their good.

*A bit of reflection:*

What are you doing to equip your children, giving them the tools to deal with stress and having a parent with a mental health challenge?

How often do you have a family meeting and discuss what's going on with family dynamics?

## Chapter 24

# When Your Child or Teen Has a Mental Illness

Many unique challenges and issues exist when the one you love who has a mental health challenge is your child or teen. Not only are you caring for them and their mental health, but also at the same time you continue to parent them. Usually, a mental health challenge for a child or teen shows up as behavioral issues. A lot of 'detective' work can be necessary in order to figure out when behavioral issues are actually the symptoms of an underlying mental health issues. Of course, all of this is made even more complex when your child/teen behaves defiantly dependent toward you.

> **Unique challenges exist when loving your child or teen**

While much of what we have said in this book about caring for yourself is applicable even if you are the parent, it is also important to note specific complexities that are part of loving and parenting your child and/or teen who has a mental health issue. Therefore, if the one you love who has a mental health challenge is a child or teen, we would recommend you check out the following resources:

**Books**

- *Grace for the Children: Finding Hope in the Midst of Child and Adolescent Mental Illness* by Matthew S. Stanford – Available in paperback and Kindle on Amazon.

- ***Mental Health and the Church: A Ministry Handbook for Including Children and Adults with ADHD, Anxiety, Mood Disorders, and Other Common Mental Health Conditions*** by Stephen Grcevich – Available in paperback and Kindle on Amazon.

## Support Groups

- **Fresh Hope for Teens and Parents** – FreshHope4Teens.com

- **Facebook community**: *Parents of Children with Mental Health Disorders Support Group* – A community of educators, caregivers, family members, friends, and the public; dedicated to educating those who suffer with Mental Health Disorders.

- **Facebook groups**: Search 'Parents of Children with Mental Health Disorders' for private group options you can request to join

## Organizations

- **Administration for Community Living (ACL) Support for Caregivers** – https://www.caregiver.org/
  ACL programs and councils help support and empower those caring for older adults and people with disabilities, which includes individuals with mental illnesses. While some of the information is targeted toward caregivers of elderly loved ones, many of the resources remain relevant and can be helpful to those providing care and support for loved ones with mental illness.

- The **American Academy of Child and Adolescent Psychiatry** – aacap.org
  Excellent resources for families: resource centers on ADHD, anxiety, bipolar disorder, depression, trauma, suicide, and many other topics. Each AACAP Resource Center contains consumer-friendly definitions, answers to frequently asked questions, clinical resources, expert videos, abstracts

from the Academy's journal, the *Scientific Proceedings*, and Facts for Families relevant to each disorder.
- o **Resource Centers** aacap.org/AACAP/Families_and_Youth/Resource_Centers/Home.aspx
- o **Facts for Families** – The Academy's Facts for Families are more concise, blog-length articles covering a broad range of topics pertaining to relevant mental health concerns for children and teens aacap.org/AACAP/Families_and_Youth/Facts_for_Families/Layout/FFF_Guide-01.aspx
- o *Journal – The Scientific Proceedings of the 66th Annual Meeting of the American Academy of Child & Adolescent Psychiatry* jaacap.org/issue/S0890-8567(19)X0002-7

- **American Psychological Association** – Search publications at apa.org Lists of resources for family members https://www.apa.org/pi/about/publications/caregivers/practice-settings/intervention/mental-illness

- **ARCH National Respite Network and Resource Center** – https://archrespite.org
  Assists and promotes the development of quality respite and crisis care programs in the United States; helps families locate respite and crisis care services in their communities; and serves as a strong voice for respite in all forums.

- **The Child Mind Institute** – childmind.org
  Provides well-written, evidence-based information for families on a wide variety of mental health topics pertaining to kids and families, with new resources published weekly.

- **Erika's Lighthouse** – erikaslighthouse.org/
  A Beacon of Hope for Adolescent Depression. Effective school-based teen depression awareness programs promoting conversations, help-seeking and empowerment — at no cost, ever.

- **The JED Foundation** – jedfoundation.org/what-we-do/families-communities/
  Excellent resources pertaining to mental health issues in teens and young adults, with a significant focus on suicide prevention and successful transitioning of teens with mental health concerns into adulthood.

- **Mental Health America (MHA) Caregiver Basics** – mhanational.org
  Information, forms, and documents that assist caregivers in providing support to their loved ones with mental illness. The tools they include help caregivers encourage loved one to become as involved as possible in their treatment, experience more in control, and work toward becoming as independent as possible. Search: Caregiver Basics.

- **National Alliance on Mental Illness (NAMI) Family Members and Caregivers** – nami.org/
  The National Alliance on Mental Illness is a leading voice for family and loved ones of individuals with mental illness. Family-to-Family is a free, 12-session educational program for family, significant others, and friends of people with mental health conditions. One of the best resources available is the NAMI Basics class (free and online), a class for parents/caregivers for children and adolescents who have a mental health diagnosis. Search: Family Members and Caregivers.

- **The Neurosequential Network** – neurosequential.com/
  Developed by Bruce D. Perry, MD, PhD, this is a biologically-respectful approach that integrates core principles of neurodevelopment and traumatology. It develops and disseminates innovative programs and practice to improve life for children, families, and communities.

- **SAMHSA (Substance Abuse and Mental Health Services Administration–** samhsa.gov

    Resources for families coping with mental and substance use disorders, Very helpful is the guide to helping a loved one experiencing mental or substance use disorder and the guide on how to start a conversation when a loved one is experiencing a mental or substance use disorder. Search: Resources for Families

## Ministries

- **Chronic Joy Chronic Illness Ministry –** chronic-joy.org

    A global resource ministry dedicated to compassionately serving all those affected by chronic illness, chronic pain, mental illness, and disability. Great resources in their Caregiving section: chronic-joy.org/caregiving.

- **Clarity Child Guidance Center –** claritycgc.org

    The only nonprofit mental health treatment center for kids ages 3 to 17 in South Texas. When a child is in crisis, they work with families to get much needed treatment regardless of their ability to pay.

- **KEY Ministry –** keyministry.org

    Helps churches minister to families of children, teens, and adults impacted by mental illness, trauma, and developmental disabilities. Provides in-person and online support resources in your special-needs parenting journey.

- **SOAR –** soarspecialneeds.org/

    SOAR Special Needs empowers families with special needs to SOAR in their local and faith communities. Families who have children with special needs face major challenges. SOAR is determined to walk beside them so that those challenges will not prevent them from obtaining a bright future.

- **To Write Love On Her Arms** – twloha.com
  TWLOHA is a non-profit movement dedicated to presenting hope and finding help for people struggling with depression, addiction, self-injury, and suicide. TWLOHA exists to encourage, inform, inspire, and also to invest directly into treatment and recovery.

**Fresh Hope Podcasts**

- **Interview with Dr. Steve Grcevich, President of Key Ministry**
  freshhopeformentalhealth.com/interview-with-dr-steve-grcevich-president-of-key-ministry/
  Dr. Grcevich is an author and physician specializing in Child and Adolescent Psychiatry. They discuss his book and model for a mental health/trauma inclusion ministry in churches of all sizes.

- **Teenagers and Mental Health**
  freshhopeformentalhealth.com/teenagers-and-mental-health/
  In this edition, Pastor Brad Hoefs interviews Dr. Brian Lubberstedt, a board certified child and adolescent psychiatrist. They discuss how mental health issues manifest in a teen's life.

- **Children and Mental Health from a Doctor's Perspective**
  freshhopeformentalhealth.com/children-mental-health-doctors-perspective/
  In this edition of Fresh Hope for Mental Health, Pastor Brad Hoefs interviews Dr. Brian Lubberstedt, who is a board certified child and adolescent psychiatrist. They discuss how potential mental health issues manifest in a child's life, parenting children who have mental health issues and much more.

- **Kids and Mental Health**
  freshhopeformentalhealth.com/kids-and-mental-health/
  Dr. Matt Stanford speaks with Pastor Brad Hoefs about his book, *Grace for the Children, Finding Hope in the Midst of Child and Adolescent Mental Illness*. We also hear about hope coaching, what it is, and how trained hope coaches can help others.

- **Groundbreaking Work in Changing Children's Severe Behavioral Issues**
  freshhopeformentalhealth.com/groundbreaking-work-in-changing-childrens-severe-behavioral-issues/
  In this edition, Pastor Brad interviews the owner of Daybreak Behavior, Mark Housman and the Clinical Director of Daybreak Behavior, Robin Houser.

*A bit of reflection:*

What unique challenge exists when your loved one is a child or teen?

A mental health challenge almost always displays as a _____ _____ in children and teens.

What out-of-the-normal behavioral issues have you seen in your child/teen?

## Chapter 25

# When Your Loved One is Suicidal

Suicide is a monster of its own kind. Feelings of anger, disbelief, sadness, and questions of 'why', and 'what ifs' will flood you.

If you are worried that your loved one may be suicidal, speak up! Don't hold it in and worry about it. Talk to them. If you have access to their doctor or therapist, call; and/or encourage your loved one to call them.

**Speak up!**

Whatever you do, talk! Talk with your loved one about it. It will not make them more suicidal.

> *"Talking to a friend or family member about their suicidal thoughts and feelings can be extremely difficult for anyone. But if you're unsure whether someone is suicidal, the best way to find out is to ask. You can't make a person suicidal by showing that you care. In fact, giving a suicidal person the opportunity to express his or her feelings can provide relief from loneliness and pent-up negative feelings, and may prevent a suicide attempt."*

Source: *HelpGuide.org*

*Ways to start a conversation about suicide:*

- "I have been feeling concerned about you lately."
- "Recently, I have noticed some differences in you and wondered how you are doing."
- "I wanted to check in with you because you haven't seemed yourself lately."

*Questions you can ask:*

- "When did you begin feeling like this?"
- "Did something happen to make you start feeling this way?"
- "How can I best support you right now?"
- "Have you thought about getting help?"

*What you can say that helps:*

- "You are not alone in this. I'm here for you."
- "You may not believe it now, but the way you're feeling will change."
- "I may not be able to understand exactly how you feel, but I care about you and want to help."
- "When you want to give up, tell yourself you will hold off for just one more day, one more hour, even one more minute—whatever you can manage."

**Risk factors**

According to the U.S. Department of Health and Human Services, at least 90 percent of all people who die by suicide suffer from one or more mental disorders such as depression, bipolar disorder, schizophrenia, or alcoholism. Depression in particular plays a large role in suicide. The difficulty that suicidal people have imagining a solution to their suffering is due in part to the distorted thinking caused by depression.

*Common suicide risk factors include:*

- Mental illness, alcoholism or drug abuse
- Previous suicide attempts, family history of suicide, or history of trauma or abuse
- Terminal illness or chronic pain
- A recent loss or stressful life event
- Social isolation and loneliness
- Antidepressants and suicide

For some, depression medication causes an increase – rather than a decrease – in depression and suicidal thoughts and feelings. Because of this risk, the FDA advises that anyone taking antidepressants should be watched for increases in suicidal thoughts and behaviors. Monitoring is especially important if this is the person's first time on depression medication, or if the dose has recently been changed. **The risk of suicide is the greatest during the first two months of antidepressant treatment.**

*The warning signs:*

- Talking about suicide – Any talk about suicide, dying, or self-harm, such as "I wish I hadn't been born," "If I see you again…" or "I'd be better off dead."
- Seeking out lethal means – Seeking access to guns, pills, knives, or other objects that could be used in a suicide attempt.

- Preoccupation with death – Unusual focus on death, dying, or violence. Writing poems or stories about death.

- No hope for the future – Feelings of helplessness, hopelessness, and being trapped ("There's no way out"). Believing that things will never get better or change.

- Self-loathing, Self-hatred – Feelings of worthlessness, guilt, shame, and self-hatred. Feeling like a burden ("Everyone would be better off without me").

- Getting affairs in order – Making out a will. Giving away prized possessions. Making arrangements for family members.

- Saying goodbye – Unusual or unexpected visits or calls to family and friends. Saying goodbye to people as if they won't be seeing them again.

- Withdrawing from others – Withdrawing from friends and family. Increasing social isolation. Desire to be left alone.

- Self-destructive behavior – Increased alcohol or drug use, reckless driving, unsafe sex. Taking unnecessary risks as if they have a "death wish."

- Sudden sense of calm – A sudden sense of calm and happiness after being extremely depressed can mean that the person has made a decision to attempt suicide.

In addition to the general risk factors for suicide, older adults and teens are at a higher risk of suicide. The highest suicide rates of any age group occur among persons aged 65 years and older. One contributing factor is depression in the elderly that is undiagnosed and untreated.

***Additional warning signs that an elderly person may be contemplating suicide:***

- Reading material about death and suicide

- Disruption of sleep patterns

- Increased alcohol or prescription drug use
- Failure to take care of self or follow medical orders
- Stockpiling medications or sudden interest in firearms
- Social withdrawal, elaborate good-byes, rush to complete or revise a will

*Source: University of Florida*

## *Risk factors for suicide in the elderly include:*

- Recent death of a loved one, isolation and loneliness
- Physical illness, disability, or pain
- Major life changes, such as retirement or loss of independence
- Loss of sense of purpose

Teenage suicide is a serious and growing problem. The teenage years can be emotionally turbulent and stressful. Teenagers face pressures to succeed and fit in. They may struggle with self-esteem issues, self-doubt, and feelings of alienation. For some, this leads to suicide. Depression is also a major risk factor for teen suicide.

## *Other risk factors for teenage suicide include:*

- Childhood abuse
- Recent traumatic event
- Lack of a support network
- Availability of a gun
- Hostile social or school environment
- Exposure to other teen suicides

*Additional warning signs that a teen may be considering suicide:*

- Change in eating and sleeping habits
- Withdrawal from friends, family, and regular activities
- Violent or rebellious behavior, running away
- Drug and alcohol use
- Unusual neglect of personal appearance
- Persistent boredom, difficulty concentrating, or a decline in the quality of schoolwork
- Frequent complaints about physical symptoms, often related to emotions, such as stomachaches, headaches, fatigue, etc.
- Rejecting praise or rewards

*Source: American Academy of Child & Adolescent Psychiatry*

*When talking to a suicidal person:*

**Do:**

- Be yourself.
- Listen. Let the suicidal person unload despair, vent anger. No matter how negative the conversation seems, the fact that it is taking place is a positive sign.
- Be sympathetic, non-judgmental, patient, calm, accepting.
- Offer hope.
- Take the person seriously.

## But don't:

- Argue with the suicidal person. Avoid saying things like: "You have so much to live for," "Your suicide will hurt your family," or "Look on the bright side."

- Act shocked, lecture on the value of life, or say that suicide is wrong.

- Promise confidentiality. Refuse to be sworn to secrecy.

- Offer ways to fix their problems, or give advice, or make them feel like they have to justify their suicidal feelings.

- Blame yourself. You can't "fix" someone's depression.

*Source: Metanoia.org*

If your loved one is living in your home, you must take safety measures to assure they do not have access to guns or other lethal means. It has shocked us through the years of how many people have been worried about their loved ones, but have not removed dangerous items like guns out of their home.

> *'A suicidal person may not ask for help, but that doesn't mean that help isn't wanted. People who take their lives don't want to die — they just want to stop hurting. Suicide prevention starts with recognizing the warning signs and taking them seriously. If you think a friend or family member is considering suicide, you might be afraid to bring up the subject. But talking openly about suicidal thoughts and feelings can save a life.'*

*Source: HelpGuide.org*
*Authors: Melinda Smith, M.A., Jeanne Segal, Ph.D., and Lawrence Robinson. Last updated: October 2019. Used by Permission of HelpGuide.org.*

This information for the most part was taken from https://www.helpguide.org/articles/suicide-prevention/suicide-prevention.htm and we encourage you to download the PDF brochure from our website at https://www.freshhope.us/

SAHMSA also has a Suicide Warning Signs wallet card you can download at https://store.samhsa.gov/system/files/sma11-disaster-11.pdf

*A bit of reflection:*

What signs have you seen in your loved one that make you suspect they might be experiencing suicidal thoughts?

As you read the list of what not to do when talking with a suicidal loved one, which reactions have you experienced? What can you do instead?

## Chapter 26

# When "I" Becomes "We" Wellness Happens

(Brad)

From my perspective, finding at least one person to trust can be key for successful recovery. Let's be honest, an untreated mental health issue can distort your loved one's perception of reality and easily affect their behavior and choices. And when this happens, they need someone to speak into their situation to help them make the necessary corrections in the course of their mental health recovery.

For me, this person has been my wife. It took me a while to believe that she was truly on 'my side' and to truly trust that she always had my best interest in mind. I'm blessed and fortunate to have a spouse who understands and is trustworthy. I realize this is not true for everyone who is married or has a partner. And if you are single, it can be a challenge to find that one trustworthy friend.

**Finding one person to trust can be key**

But I'm convinced that having this 'one person' in my life has enabled me to get past the 'i' of illness. When I allowed my wife to begin to be a partner in my recovery, we moved to 'we'. When you replace the 'i' of 'illness' with 'we', the result is 'wellness'. And that is what I experienced and continue to experience – mental wellness.

Now as you would expect, we do not always agree. And when that happens, we have an agreement that I bring it to the attention of the doctor at my next appointment, or if it's of a more urgent nature, then I call him. This has happened only a few times in the past fifteen years. One time my doctor confirmed Donna's concern, and the other times he confirmed my point of view. Sometimes my wife's concerns are based more upon her fear of my relapsing than upon actual bipolar issues, something she acknowledges.

Now, this 'one-person' needs to be:
- someone they fully trust and feel completely safe with
- someone who believes in them
- someone who wants to see them succeed
- someone who believes that they can live well in spite of having a mental illness
- someone who will listen and understand them, but also challenge them to push through when it would be easier to give up
- someone who would be willing to go along with them to their doctor appointment from time to time
- someone who will hold them accountable, who can ask the hard questions that are key for their recovery
- someone who has access to their doctor and therapist
- someone who has a fairly good understanding of mental illness but is willing to learn a lot more and become as informed as is possible about the challenge and their journey in particular

- someone who knows them and is part of their daily life
- someone that your loved one is willing to allow to 'speak into' their recovery

*A bit of reflection:*

Does your loved one have someone who can take the 'i' out of illness and make it 'we', moving to wellness? If not, how can you help them find such a person? We encourage you to identify such a person and bring them onto your team.

In the list above, in which areas do you feel unable to help your loved one?

## Chapter 27

# 30 Things You Can Do When Someone You Love is Clinically Depressed

When you love someone that is experiencing deep depression, it can be exhausting and frustrating. You want to encourage your loved one, but don't want to push them too much. Encouraging them to 'push through' but knowing when to do so is a delicate balance. You might even find yourself emotionally feeling their depression. No doubt, caring for someone who is in the depths of depression can feel as though life is being sucked out of you. You can end up having no idea how to help or encourage your loved one.

> **It's a delicate balance**

*Here are some things my wife did for me and/or encouraged me to do when I was in the depths of depression:*

1. Encourage them to do something that they have enjoyed doing in the past, and do it with them.

2. Watch an uplifting movie together.

3. Cook their favorite meal.

4. Sit quietly with them. Hold their hand.

5. Take a walk together.

### 30 Things You Can Do When Someone You Love is Clinically Depressed

6. Take care of yourself!

7. Help them establish and stick to a schedule.

8. Have some expectations of them.

9. Assure them of your unconditional love.

10. Assure them that this will pass – sooner or later.

11. Give a back rub.

12. Listen to soothing, spiritually uplifting music with them.

13. Ask them to help you make or do something.

14. Encourage them to talk, and listen carefully to them when they do.

15. Encourage them to see a doctor if they have not done so, and to keep their appointments.

16. Assure them you don't believe that they are weak or lack faith, but that you know their brain chemistry is experiencing imbalance.

17. Ask them to promise you that if they ever begin to feel suicidal that they will tell you immediately. If they tell you, consult with their doctor as soon as possible or contact the Suicide Hotline at 800.273.8255. If the situation is an emergency, dial 911.

18. Ask them what might bring them comfort.

19. Talk about the future. Help them to see there is a future.

20. Encourage them to exercise with you.

21. Turn on the lights, open the windows.

22. Learn as much as you can about depression. This is a great website: lighterblue.com/#lighter-blue.

23. Change your light bulbs to full spectrum light bulbs.

24. Give your loved one a mood light. Northern Light Technologies [northernlighttechnologies.com] is one company with a wide variety of options. (Check with the doctor before purchasing these.)

25. Get them Vitamin D and $B_{12}$.

26. Remind them of times when they have overcome adversity so they know it is possible for them to do so again.

27. Encourage them to get outside for a walk and some natural sunlight.

28. Turn off news programs and other negative media. Control negative inputs.

29. Where possible, encourage them to connect with friends.

30. Pray. Every time you find yourself worrying about your loved one, pray instead.

Please know, as a loved one it is SO important that you do take care of yourself as well. Stay balanced and do some things that you enjoy. Take care of yourself spiritually and emotionally. Also, know this, the Lord is with you, too! He will see you through this valley. Stay in His word. Hold to His hope. And when you can, laugh a little! You are not alone. There is hope. And there is healing.

### *A bit of reflection:*

Identify and note 7 of the 30 above suggestions that you have or are currently doing for your loved one.

Select 3-5 suggestions from the list that you can start doing this week.

Why is it important for you, as the loved one, to take care of your own physical, spiritual, and emotional well-being, especially while caring for your loved one?

# Chapter 28

# The Power of Peers Helping Peers

Throughout the United States and several other countries, a movement is occurring in which states are certifying peers to help peers. It's called Certified Peer Support Specialists. They're not licensed certifications, but are programs and certifications which the state establishes. A peer is defined in this situation as someone who has or is living an experience with mental illness. The research shows that peers get as much help from a peer helping them as from a therapist, and in some cases even more.

It can be an extremely positive experience if your loved one can find a Certified Peer Support Specialist, someone they can really connect with who can help them in their recovery. At the time of writing this book, Fresh Hope is establishing training and certification for Hope Navigators, which is our version of Peer Support Specialists. Check with our international office to see if we have a Hope Coach or Hope Navigator that your loved one can take advantage of. There's great power when peers help peers.

> **There's great power when peers help peers**

For instance, Brad can say things to another person with a mental health challenge that someone who's never had a mental health challenge can't say. And there are things that the doctor and therapist can't say, but a peer can say to another peer.

Peers can be there for one another 24/7, something else a doctor or therapist can't do. When looking at the power of peer-to-peer support, think what can happen within a peer-led group such as Fresh Hope. This is extremely powerful when a group of peers come together, and the environment is such that there's direction and movement towards taking their lives in a positive way. It is certainly our hope that every Fresh Hope group is helpful. But beware of groups that are only venting groups, that have no purpose to move towards improved lives.

Fresh Hope is not a venting group. For instance, our meetings focus on a topic, we apply the tenets to our lives, there's direction towards healing and recovery, and are very hope driven. That's not true of all mental health support groups. If you have groups in your community that aren't Fresh Hope, watch carefully, because when people only vent in a mental health support group, they will get sicker. What do I mean by venting? It means you come every week and just dump everything out and talk about how awful things are. What happens is people actually build upon it and become increasingly negative. You don't see any good; all you can see is the bad. And in my personal perspective, that's one way that people start to become chronically mentally ill.

But if you can find a peer-led mental health support group like Fresh Hope, a group that's positive, encouraging, empowering, and hope-driven, it can be so powerful in helping your loved one succeed in their recovery. If you don't have a Fresh Hope group in your area, you can participate in an online group. Another suggestion is to enlist a group of peers or a trusted individual who will support and encourage your loved one. From Brad's perspective, it's a major factor for people recovering and living well in spite of a mental health diagnosis. Never underestimate the power of a hope-filled, living-well peer!

Remember, finding a hope-filled mental health group can be one of the major keys in your loved one learning to live well in spite of their mental health challenge.

## *A bit of reflection:*

What advantages does a peer support specialist provide that you can't?

Is your loved one is open to connecting with a Certified Peer Support Specialist? Ask their doctor for a recommendation, do an online search for 'Peer Support Specialists near me', or contact the Fresh Hope International office to get connected with a Hope Navigator.

What is the difference between a 'venting' support group and one that equips, as Fresh Hope groups do?

# Recommended Resources

- **Fresh Hope for Mental Health** www.FreshHope.us
  Support Groups locally and online, Podcasts, Blog Posts, Videos, and numerous other free resources.

- *Fresh Hope: Living Well in Spite of a Mental Health Diagnosis: A Wellness Workbook for Fresh Hope* by Brad Hoefs
  This is Pastor Brad's first book, explaining Fresh Hope and the Principles of Recovery.
  Available at www.freshhope.us/product/1-fresh-hope-book/ and on Amazon.

- **Fresh Hope Principles of Recovery** https://www.freshhope.us/our-story/#fh-tenets
  The complete list, including Part 1 of each principle for the person with the diagnosis.

- **Trauma Healing Institute** (American Bible Institute) thi.americanbible.org/
  Trauma happens when a person is overwhelmed with fear, helplessness, or horror in the face of death. This affects their psychological, physical, emotional, and spiritual well-being. *How do people recover from trauma? Can the Bible help? What can the church do?* Trauma Healing is our response to these questions. Contact https://www.freshhope.us/fh-groups/ to schedule a class.

- *Grace for the Afflicted: A Clinical and Biblical Perspective on Mental Illness* by Matthew S. Stanford
  Why has the church struggled in ministering to those with mental illnesses? This book is written to educate Christians about mental illness from both Biblical and scientific perspectives. Describing common mental disorders, Dr. Stanford probes what science says and what the Bible says about each illness.

- *Troubled Minds: Mental Illness and the Church's Mission* by Amy Simpson
  Too often we reduce people who are mentally ill to caricatures and ghosts, and pretend they don't exist. And then there are their friends and family members, who bear their own scars and anxious thoughts, and who see no safe place to talk about the impact of mental illness on their lives and their loved ones. This book reminds us that people with mental illness are our brothers and sisters in Christ, and shows us the path to loving them well and becoming a church that loves God with whole hearts and whole souls.

- **Good Therapy** www.goodtherapy.org
  Millions of people use Good Therapy to find therapists and counselors, rehab and residential treatment centers, and mental health resources. Good Therapy believes that with the right support, anyone is capable of healing, growth, and change.

- **NAMI FaithNet** www.nami.org/namifaithnet
  An interfaith resource network of NAMI members, friends, clergy, and congregations of all faith traditions who wish to encourage faith communities who are welcoming and supportive of persons and families living with mental illness.

CPSIA information can be obtained
at www.ICGtesting.com
Printed in the USA
LVHW050718060821
694569LV00004B/10